HOW TO RUN A BOUTIQUE YOYO BUSINESS

J.D. McKay

Cover designed by Waylon Crase and Andra McKay
Comics by Stephanie Honeycutt
Yoyo Diagrams by Cameron Blair

I am neither a lawyer nor accountant. Statements in this book are suggested start points, not actual legal advice. Please consult legal professionals in your area for any and all legal and tax questions.

J.D. McKay
Visit my website at www.jdmckay.com

First Printing: Aug. 2019

For information about bulk purchases, sales, promotions, fundraising, and education needs, please contact J.D. McKay at jdmckayauthor@gmail.com

ISBN-978-1-9991887-0-2

Table of Contents

FOREWORD

BY ANDRA MCKAY

Those who know him know that J.D. is a deeply kind man, as well as quite extraordinarily and delightfully weird. It is a privilege to be supportive of his passion for yoyo. Yes, we negotiated that he would at least remove the ever-present yoyo from his belt during our wedding ceremony, but I couldn't be prouder than when he graciously does tricks for yet another random stranger I've been talking to about him.

His journey in the yo-yo world has been something I've had the honor to watch over the past seven and a half years. In that time he has transitioned from sponsored player and YouTube teacher, to company division manager, to online store owner, and finally to the creator of a truly unique brand that focuses on creativity and collaboration. It is an inspiration to watch. His biggest strength is his ability to bring together a diverse group of people with his sense of fun. He is an inspiration to me.

Along the way he also racked up a couple of Canadian championships in off-string yoyo. He has spent countless hours showing children and adults alike how to throw. We've travelled to far flung cities we wouldn't have otherwise visited, such as Reykjavik, Prague, and Cleveland.

We jokingly refer to me as his manager (well, I did help negotiate his rate as a technical advisor on a TV show), but really what I am is his biggest fan. I hope after reading this book (and his wacky Duckpocalypse book) that you'll be a fan too.

INTRODUCTION

Ahh, that famous "How hard could it be?" question. The sound of bigger-than-expected projects devouring small business owners the world over. The entrepreneur mentality isn't for everyone and running your own small business is hard work. Still, it can be extremely rewarding — especially, when you provide something that brings people many hours of joy and fulfillment. Like a yoyo, for example.

A little about me. I'm a man of many hats, both literally and figuratively (waaaay too many Tribys in my closet). I'm a musician, a basketball player, a writer, a yoyo performer, and a teacher. I was once a competitive yoyoer but retired from competition to spend more time being creative and less time training. My "day job" is that of an elementary school teacher, and I love it. It was, in fact, this job that led me to yoyos. An organization called The Ned Show made an appearance at a school assembly, delivering an inspirational storytelling yoyo performance. They sold yoyos to the kids, and I bought one so I could learn enough to help the kids out. Yoyos were everywhere, and I was hooked!

Ten years later, I doubt that any of those kids still play with their yoyos, but I'm still going strong. I founded the Canadian Yoyo Association and have organized or helped organize over a dozen contests at the provincial, regional, or national level. I've won two Canadian Yoyo Championship titles and competed at the world contest. I've taught thousands of people how to yoyo either in person or through the hundreds of tutorials on my YouTube channel.

I find myself in the position of being someone yoyoers come to for advice when starting their own brand, so it makes sense to get it down in writing. I will begin with a disclaimer. I have a university degree in history and education. My business degree is from the University of Trial and Error, Fail Before You Succeed department. I have read books, consulted with experts on business and marketing, and made a lot of mistakes. I've been a sponsored player, run an online retail store, and been the manager of someone else's brand. I currently head a successful brand (Rain City Skills) that is on its way to being a well-known name in the industry, with a stable fan base and a back catalogue of successful releases.

All these experiences have put me in a position where I can share knowledge about the way the yoyo world works. We live in an era of lowered barriers between creators and their customers, and with that an explosion of boutique brands have entered the market. This book represents the accumulated knowledge, skills, and understanding I've acquired over the years. It's by no means a complete guide to getting rich selling yoyos. What it will do is (1) give yoyoers reading it a glimpse into the origin of their yoyo and (2) provide boutique brand owners with a toolkit of tricks to help build their brands.

What Is a Boutique Yoyo Company?

Not long ago, a boutique yoyo brand's only real option for sales was through either an online or a brick-and-mortar retail store. Before services like PayPal and Square made online payments easy and safe, it just wasn't feasible to handle managing a webstore, accepting payments, and shipping out products all by yourself. Today, it's easy to build a web store or even sell directly through sites like Facebook.

For the purposes of this book, I'm going to divide the yoyo industry into three broad categories: the boutique brand, the small brand, and the big brand.

I define a boutique company as one that is run by an individual, who releases yoyos in small batches with limited numbers. These brands are usually available only directly or through select online retail stores.

A small brand handles larger volume and restocks its main models. It likely has a worldwide customer base. Often, a small brand still revolves around a single operator/owner, who handles the process from beginning to end but may have a part-time employee to help out.

A big brand tends to have one or more "flagship" lines it keeps in stock online and in retail stores. The brand doesn't necessarily center around one person, as their volume is large enough to warrant various managers (say, sales and/or shipping) or other employees.

These are not comprehensive definitions; rather, they give us a framework to work with. At the time of writing, I still categorize my company, Rain City Skills, as boutique, but it is growing rapidly towards a small brand status. I don't know whether I ever want it to grow into a big worldwide business. We'll see what the future holds.

Traditionally, the yoyo business was limited to companies with money to spend, as start-up costs could be prohibitive. If you go back fifteen years, machined aluminum yoyos were hard to source, and today's quality standards were near unachievable. Today, start-up costs are lower, access to services is much wider, and demand is growing. This has led to the rise of dozens of "boutique" yoyo companies.

When I started yoyoing in 2009, there were fewer brands on the market than there are now. I remember having a very reasonable goal of acquiring a yoyo from each of the dozen or so brands operating in North America. In 2019, there are more than fifty boutique yoyo brands in the same market. On top of that, we have string makers and accessory brands — all of which tell a tale of a very busy time for yoyo!

This book is a guide for those of you starting your journey into yoyo creation, for those who have been at it a while and are looking for some new perspective, and for the community at large who want to know where their yoyos come from. I walk you through creating and marketing a brand; managing social media; designing, advertising, and selling your yoyos. My book isn't a recipe for guaranteed wealth and fame, but it's a starting point that you can use to launch into you own brand of success.

Part I is an overview of my business history and what I've learned from both successes and failures. This works as both a résumé and a practical example of the information in Parts II and III.

Part II examines the planning you need to do around marketing. I present a variety of tools and strategies that you have at your disposal.

Part III outlines the steps in getting a yoyo made, some of the costs and the challenges you may face, and ways to make sure you have the best chance of getting a quality product.

Setting Goals

What is it about making a yoyo that gets you excited? The act of designing? Planning the colors? The thought of seeing other people playing with your creation? Imagined piles of money from your record-breaking sales? That last one isn't likely, but you never know! The rest of them are all good reasons to consider making yoyos. If you are a yoyo enthusiast getting into the industry, make sure you do it for personally fulfilling reasons. Be careful your joy for the hobby doesn't get drowned in the mundane grind of running a business.

Why start a yoyo brand? What is your end goal? This is a really important thing to know from the get-go. Do you want to

1. Become the biggest name in the yoyo business with products in big chain retail stores,

2. Find a nice comfortable spot in the middle of the pack, releasing a couple of yoyos a year,

3. Make that one yoyo you have been dreaming about for a year and then stop?

Find the middle point between what you want to make and what you can actually sell. Releasing an old-fashioned wood yoyo is great if it's your passion, but how many people are going to buy one? If you have done your research and have customers lined up, you might be looking at a viable product. If not, consider creating something with more reach.

If being the biggest is your goal, you need to begin as a business manager who happens to make yoyos. If you are looking to sit in the middle of the pack, you can start small and grow. If your goal is to make a beautiful piece of art, consider how much work you want to put into the business. You might be better off approaching an established brand, with an idea and fistfuls of cash to finance it.

The act of starting one's own yoyo brand is a very large leap of faith. It is a small industry with very small profit margins. Designing and prototyping takes time and money. Competition, social media management, sponsoring players, and getting your product just right are only some of the challenges you will face. Very few companies generate enough revenue to make it past the single owner/operator stage. The few that do end up with, at most, one or two employees. Once the owner decides to call it quits, the product line dies. One bad run (machining errors, color problems, etc.) can wipe out a start-up.

My personal goal is to find a nice comfortable place in the middle of the pack. I don't need to be an industry dominating force like the Duncan yoyo brand, but I do want to create a business that lets me express my creativity while providing at least a little bit of income

Guiding Principles

Here are three ideas I recommend you consider before getting started.

First, who are you? Find a way to reflect on who YOU are in your business. Have a story to tell. In a market where it's hard to make a bad yoyo, you need to give potential customers a reason to choose yours over the competition. Copying another brand's strategy (marketing, style, etc.) is going to be an uphill battle. People will be less likely to connect with your project if it doesn't seem to be genuine. This is a small community, and we talk to each other. If you do something you believe in, people are more likely to support you.

Second, have you shown integrity? Can you be relied on to keep your word, follow through with a task, or own up to a mistake? I've interacted with a lot of great people in the yoyo business. Kind, generous, and enthusiastic people. Unfortunately, some of them can also be unreliable. Priorities shift; day jobs and families can take precedence. But it makes them harder to work with. If I'm relying on an email reply from someone so I can move forward with a project, waiting is difficult. If I've invested money in a project on the promise of someone's contribution, the project can be set back or fall apart completely if they don't come through in time. I recommend making a practice of doing everything in your power to keep your word when you give it, and if you can't, communicate fast so your business partners are able to come up with other arrangements.

Third, do you have the resources to complete your project? Or are you stretching beyond your means? This could refer to finances. (What if the entire run of yoyos is flawed and you have to start over?) It can also refer to time and energy. (Can you keep on top of email communication, ship on time, etc.). The yoyo market has its ups and downs (pun intended), and you need to prepare for the worst. You can recover from a mishap and move forward if you've left yourself room to adapt.

There is much more to being ready to run a business, but these pillars have made a strong foundation for my business and afforded me a position of respect and support from my customers and community. I believe they will do the same for you.

A small business isn't a surefire way to make a living and is usually far more work for reward than a nine-to-five job is. Long hours, hard work, and financial risk are what you get in the beginning. If you are just looking to make money, get a job working for someone else. It's a lot easier. I know I have to sell thirty yoyos for the profits to equal what I make in one day teaching. But I really enjoy this business, so the rewards for me go beyond financial. If you have passion and desire, you can make a success of it. And, hopefully, have some fun along the way!

If you have decided that running a business is what you want to do, then this book will start you on the right track.

MY BUSINESS

JOURNEY

My first glimpse into the inner workings of the manufacturing end of the yoyo world came when I had the privilege of being sponsored by MonkeyfingeR Design. They provided me with yoyos, and in exchange I used exclusively their products for competitions or making videos. They got advertising, and I got to be part of a brand with an occasional exclusive yoyo. I became good friends with Ray Smith, the company's owner, and so I got to talk to him a lot about how his company had grown. I was on the team from near the beginning to the point where he had a solid foothold in the market. My year on his team was invaluable. It's where I got started making video tutorials, which remains one of my main marketing tools. MonkeyfingeR now has worldwide recognition and an extremely dedicated fan base. When I was running my own online retail store, MonkeyfingeR was one of the few brands I could be 100 percent sure would sell out.

Below is Ray's story. It'll give you a pretty good idea of what trying to set up your own brand may mean.

MonkeyfingeR Design

MonkeyfingeR Design all started thanks to my son. When he was about ten years old, I was looking for something that the two of us could do and learn together. After perusing YouTube for some ideas, I just happened to come across a video of some young kid showing off all five of the yoyo disciplines. For me at the time, it seemed crazy and spectacular. I was immediately intrigued. Here was something I could do with my son that wasn't a video game and required a lot of skill to learn. So, we managed to find some old-style Duncan Butterfly yoyos at a specialty shop. These yoyos seemed awesome to us at the time, and we played them for a few weeks. I then discovered another specialty shop here in Calgary, called Livingstone & Cavell, and was introduced to my first high-end yoyo from SPYY.

I will admit that I was pretty naïve at the time. Throwing yoyos should be easy, right? Needless to say, it didn't take long for me to prove myself wrong. It takes practice, a LOT of practice. Still, I was hooked and became a bit obsessed with throwing. While searching for yoyo tutorials, I discovered YoyoExpert.com, which still to this day is the big daddy of yoyo stores. I watched the tutorials. I practiced like crazy. I went to local yoyo meetings. I dove in. And somewhere in there, I started asking myself, "You know, how hard could it be to make a yoyo? It's just a yoyo!" Like I said, completely naïve.

OK, OK, I know. As any yoyo manufacturer will tell you, making a yoyo is no joke and is incredibly more complicated than it seems. Nonetheless, I did extensive research on yoyo shapes and settled on a design that I hadn't seen before. Thus, was born the very first MonkeyfingeR yoyo, the Evil-Yo. In my mind, we had something quite substantial in this design, and I began looking for machine shops who could take on the project. I think I talked to at least seven shops before finding one that would do the job. A few weeks later, I had five prototypes in my hands. MonkeyfingeR Design was now a thing!

GruntBull Anodizing was able to do the colorwork for the prototypes. Nothing fancy, just a few acid wash combos to start. I got them back, slapped some response pads on them, and excitedly took them to the next yoyo meeting to get some feedback. For the most part, the players thought the design had some promise, although it was clear that it needed some extra rim weight. It was a departure from anything they were used to, which is what I was after. A few design tweaks later, it was back to the machine shop, and away we went.

It didn't take long for me to become unhappy with the current standards for anodization. It seemed that each time I had a cool colorway (pattern of colors on the yoyo) idea, I kept hearing "Sorry we can't do that!" Lame! This left me with a bunch of yoyo parts and nobody to anodize them to my satisfaction. Well, since we managed to start a yoyo company from scratch, couldn't we also figure out anodizing from scratch? I decided to put MonkeyfingeR development on hold while I tried my hand at anodizing.

Also, at about this time, I approached one of the guys from my work who had a background in art, Todd Damboise, to see whether he would be interested in doing some MonkeyfingeR artwork. He asked me a few questions about the company and the vision. To my surprise, he offered to partner with me to work on MonkeyfingeR. Todd started working on the Evil-Yo artwork, while I tackled anodizing. We set up a minimal DIY kit for my garage and set about to testing anodization. It took us months to figure out how to correctly anodize with any amount of consistency, but we managed to crack the code!

Our first colorway was a four-color splash called Mizaru. We used this with the first official Evil-Yo release, and it was met with silence and crickets. Not the resounding success we had hoped for. To be fair, at that time the most complicated colorway was a single splash color on a solid background. We were clearly a bit ahead of our time. But we were undeterred because we felt we were on to something special. Our next colorway was the Kikazaru. Players warmed up to this one a bit more, and people seemed to be coming around to the idea of crazy colorways with *lots of bright palettes. Next came the Iwazaru colorway, and this completed our see-no-evil, hear-no-evil, speak-no-evil monkey theme. From this point, we started experimenting with all kinds of anodizing ideas: fades, swirls, speckles — you name it. Everything we could think of AND the kitchen sink!*

Perhaps I should back up the story a bit here. By this point, we had made a solid run of one hundred yoyos and anodized them all. The problem was we were greatly struggling to put them together as A-grade yoyos. We refused to release an entire run of B-grades (yoyos with flaws), so we shelved the entire batch and started searching for a higher-quality machine shop. At machine shop, number ten we found a winner. This new shop was able to make parts for another one hundred yoyos. We anodized them and sighed a huge sigh of relief when we were able to put them together to make solid and smooth A-grades yoyos. We learned a lot from that experience, although, admittedly, it cost us a huge amount of time and money.

Finally, we got a Hail Mary break from Brent, the owner of High Speed Yoyo. Brent took a chance on us and agreed to stock the Evil-Yo in his online store, which was one of the most popular online yoyo sites at the time. Then, a week later, Andre from Yoyo Expert also agreed to carry the Evil-Yo. They both took a huge risk on an unknown yoyo manufacturer that was slinging a crazy yoyo design with some crazy colorways. To this day, Andre remains supporting all our crazy ideas. The rest, as they say, is history.

It was a rough start, no doubt about it. Since then, however, MonkeyfingeR has emerged as a manufacturer of high-end yoyos with some of the best anodization work in the industry. We have gathered a huge base of loyal fans, and they have made us into the yoyo success story that we are today. I would be lying if said there weren't any moments early on that I wanted to pack it and give up. We, of course, didn't, and I am glad we stuck it out because MonkeyfingeR Design is here to stay!

Ray's story is one of challenges that led to success. His ability to find a hole in the market and fill it with a unique and cohesive brand image turned his hobby into a viable business. MonkeyfingeR Design isn't his full-time job, but it's a nice artistic outlet for him that pays for itself and then some. It took him a lot of trial and error to get it right, but he has definitely done so. My time on his team gave me a taste of the wider world of sales. But my own chance to jump into the yoyo market finally came only in the summer of 2013, and in a form very different from most others.

King Yo Star

In 2013, my wife and I decided to drive to the Canadian National Championships in Edmonton, Alberta, as an excuse for a road trip. It's a twelve-hour drive each way, but we stretched it out to a couple of weeks. After the contest, we traveled through Alberta, playing tourist (dinosaur bones, woohoo!).

That's when I received a very unexpected email from a friend with an offer to handle marketing and promotion for a yoyo brand. At the time, King Yo Star, a growing Chinese brand, was branching out into Canada. They needed a new face for the brand in Canada and the U.S., someone who would help move the small brand into the mainstream. The company would send me the yoyos and I would sell them, paying back the cost only after I completed the sales. As you've learned from Ray's story, manufacturing at that time was high cost and high risk. This offer gave me the ability to get into the market, without having to be the one carrying the financial risk.

Thus began my crash course in business. Prior to this, the extent of my business training came from the auction house in the World of Warcraft video game. While everyone else ran around slaying beasts to collect loot, I learned the patterns of what was in demand. Then I bought equipment and materials to re-list them for a profit. It got to the point where I drove the average prices on my server up to double that of others. This may seem to be a silly non sequitur until you consider the fact that the skill of studying a market and figuring out what will sell is critical to running a yoyo brand.

Sales and Marketing

The job didn't turn out to be as simple as emailing retailers to ask how many yoyos they'd like. In 2013, stores were hesitant about bringing in Chinese brands. Most North American companies were still making their yoyos in the U.S. or Canada. Chinese-made yoyos were tainted by the reputation of a few unscrupulous Chinese companies making and selling copies of other brands. This changed over time, in part because the Chinese government cracked down on copyright infringement. At one point, I had a shipment of King Yo Star yoyos held at the border until I proved that I was the "owner" of the brand. Chinese customs thought that King Yo Star China, the actual owner, was copying my brand!

During my time with King Yo Star, I learned a lot about promotion.

There is power in a name. In the beginning, I was getting the leftovers of designs made for the Chinese market. The Prober was the first yoyo I was tasked with selling. It was named by a native Chinese speaker, trying out the concept of a space probe pushing the limits of yoyo design. Obviously, they should have consulted a native English speaker first, but it worked for the Chinese market.

Colors have the power to either drive or hinder sales. When I approached online stores with the Prober and later the Kit, I was told that the purple and pink that I had to offer weren't desirable, that those colors didn't sell well in yoyos. So I filed that information away for future use.

Marketing is the biggest piece of yoyo sales. People aren't going to buy yoyos from a brand they know nothing about. At the time, the only way I knew to market yoyos was contest sponsorship and sponsored players. So I attended some. I took a chance and made the trip to the 2013 California State Yoyo contest and brought yoyos to sell. I sponsored the event, so the King Yo Star logo was on the banner, and I had an official vendor table. I made a number of new connections and had a really good time! In the years since, I've learned that nothing is more effective in sales than those personal connections. It's not just about selling one yoyo; I want customers who will buy the next twelve yoyos.

Sponsoring the Right Players

Song Yao collected some talented players during his time running King Yo Star. Over time, I found more. Later that first year, we took a big chance and sponsored Jake Elliot. Jake splashed into the competitive yoyo scene in 2013. He came out of nowhere to win the U.S. National 5a Championships. I got approval from the head of King Yo Star in China and offered Jake a flight to the world championships in Prague and his own signature yoyo. This was an expensive gamble but one that paid off in respectability and brand recognition.

This is where I got to learn about design and the risks of innovation. Jake wanted a bi-metal yoyo — one made of aluminum with stainless steel rings added to put the weight right where it would do the most good. (I'll cover the mechanics of this later.) This turned out to be a challenging project. The style was relatively rare at the time. The shop we used didn't have much experience connecting a ring of stainless steel to the aluminum body. We went through two time-consuming prototypes and weren't ready in time for the World Yoyo Championship in Prague (2014). Luckily, Jake needed only one prototype to hit a near perfect routine. He placed second that year by a tiny margin. When we eventually got the yoyo made, there was a lot of demand for it.

In late fall of 2014, we finally had a hundred made. Unfortunately, only about fifty of them were of good enough quality to sell as "A- grades" at full retail price. The rest had balance issues and were either unsellable or had to be sold at cost or lower. The benefit of having the yoyo represented by the second-ranked yoyoer in the world was that these sold out very quickly. Unfortunately, the challenge of being a boutique company is that bigger companies can make better offers, and Jake decided to make the same career decision I did when I left MFD — he moved on to work for yoyotricks.com.

The Beginning of the End

I continued to build up King Yo Star. The Rapid gave us respectability, and we moved forward with other designs. I released my first "signature" yoyo — a design with my name on it, which sold well. I was also competing seriously in the offstring style of yoyo (see appendix B). I connected with

MonkeyfingeR Ray, and we decided to make an offstring yoyo together. We called it the Silverback King, combining the two brand names.

The Silverback King was supposed to be a dream come true. When I left MonkeyfingeR Design to run King Yo Star, I promised myself that I would still collaborate with them at some point later. That time had come. I would finally have my own offstring design to compete with. I personally loved it, won the Canadian Offstring Championships with it twice, and felt that it was perfect for me. But our product ended up otherwise being an unmitigated disaster.

Neither of us had designed an offstring yoyo before, but we had some guidelines for what we wanted. I handed them off to the designer in China, who had been helping me. I gave him instructions to create a design and get back to me for approval. It should have been a knockout, as the Chinese 4a champion was involved. Instead, there was nothing but miscommunication. Months later, when I finally got a response, I learned that three prototypes had already been made and that he was sending me the fourth. Each prototype cost around US$300 to make, so this was a problem. The fourth prototype wasn't right, so we had to do a fifth. Eventually, the design hit the "as good as it's going to get" point, and it was time to produce a run of a hundred.

It was our first foray into plastics, and I made the critical mistake of failing to check that the factory had the necessary experience. You can't make an offstring yoyo out of aluminum due to the frequency with which it flies off the string and hits floor, walls, and the occasional lamp. We used a material called Delrin, which is a very dense plastic. Somewhere between the machine shop and design stage, there was a critical flaw that made those yoyos almost impossible to balance. I spent countless hours matching halves and ended up with barely fifty out of the hundred I could sell at retail prices. It was probably fifty hours of work just getting those matched up, boxed, and sold. Because of the multiple prototypes driving up our costs, we ended up selling them to stores at cost just to get some of our money back. Both MonkeyfingeR and I ended up losing money on this yoyo.

This alone might not have ended my career as the head of King Yo Star Canada, but around the same time, we released a 1a yoyo called Pax. Again, I told the designer my ideas, and then we made a prototype. It was nothing like I expected, but it was a fantastic player. It just looked odd. I went ahead with it anyway, which was a mistake. I brought samples to the Vancouver Yoyo Club meeting, and everyone loved it! But with this design, unless players could actually handle it and feel how well it played, they just looked at the weird design and took a pass. This meant I now had one hundred yoyos that weren't selling, immediately following my earlier failure.

By the end of 2015, I decided that this page of my business education was done. I'd had enough of running someone else's brand. I no longer wanted to be the middleman. If I was going to run a small yoyo company again, it would be as the head. I would wait until I had a great concept that would hook people, something that would generate the hype needed to drive sales and bring back reliable, repeat customers.

I figured this would take a while and that I'd have a break. My wife, it turned out, had other plans.

Rain City Skills

Sometimes, you have to work hard to find just the right idea to move you forward. Sometimes, these opportunities fall into your lap. Starting Rain City Skills was the logical next step in my yoyo journey and my personal growth in the business. It began as many things do — with a road trip.

Road Trip to Oregon

In August 2016, my friend Wayne Ngan travelled from Toronto to visit his family in Vancouver. He brought up the idea of doing a road trip to Eugene, Oregon, to visit the One Drop (OD) yoyo factory. We left early on a Friday morning and did the eight-hour drive in one shot. When we pulled in late in the afternoon, company owners Shawn and David greeted us warmly and gave us the tour. One Drop is unique because their shop makes almost exclusively yoyos. That wasn't always the case. Before the yoyo world walked in their door, they were paying the bills by making parts for a local BMX shop — for example, trying to create the perfect "to-go" cup mount for a bike. OD started with their own brand of yoyos but quickly opened up their shop to machining for other brands.

Today, when someone hands you a prototype yoyo, it's a completed design that may just need a few tweaks. But when they started making yoyos, it was a different story. Shawn shared with us a series of parts in various states of becoming a yoyo. These represented OD's experimental journey that became the One Drop "Project", now a sought-after collector piece. Since their humble beginnings, they've scaled up, upgraded their machinery, and are now producing world-class yoyos. One Drop reinvented the machining process from scratch. I learned a lot about the precision involved in the design during my visit. It's eye opening to see how much waste making a yoyo produces. And yet it isn't surprising when you consider how thin the body of a yoyo is. Below you see a series of test pieces One Drop worked through.

This is the photo evidence of us designing our first yoyo but also learning how to actually make one. We were using a Mill, not a lathe, which is not the correct machine, and it's not ideal. Interestingly, it led to the Project having some unique features like the nut capture and the projection profile. Something to keep in mind is that in 2007 all the companies were in the process of figuring out the best way to make modern yoyos. It was an exciting time, and that was our first contribution.

<u>Top Row:</u>
1.   Initial test. First test was to see whether we could cut a dome on the mill.
2.   The second test was making the cup side and testing the nut capture.
<u>Second row, left to right:</u>
1.   Basically taking the two initial tests and making our first playable prototype
2.   Changing to a smaller nut size and rounding the rims
3.   Changing the axle from imperial to metric and refining the hub
4.   Adding an engraving on the hub and other small refinements
5.   Moving the engraving to the rim and adding the "nibs" to the nut capture
6.   Adding more small refinements and making it slightly more narrow
<u>Bottom Row</u>
1.   Adding more small refinements and going to production. Final version.

Shawn spent the evening with us, sharing stories of the business and politics of the yoyo world, and we had a great time. Generally, they are open to having people come visit. (Just make sure to talk to them in advance.) The truth is that they didn't set out to make specifically yoyos when they went into business, but fate definitely put them there. Where MonkeyfingeR Ray's business model focuses on the way yoyos are finished, One Drop has perfected the art of carving a great yoyo out of a simple rod of aluminum.

One Drop started in 2001 as a contract machine shop while we kept our day jobs. We knew that at some point the right idea would walk through the door. It turned out to be yoyos in 2007. We made one for a student intern, and we called it The

Project. We decided to try to sell some, and it was an instant hit. We just took off from there and went full time in 2009.

The core idea of our business was to make products in our own shop in Eugene — Made in America — from the start. And we wanted products that we loved and would want as well. In the early years of yoyos, almost none were being made in China. Since then, our competitors have mostly migrated that way, leaving us as the main U.S. high-end yoyo company. It's tough to compete against the prices coming out of China, but we have stuck with our original vision and fortunately for us, there are enough customers who appreciate what we do. We will never switch to outsourcing, as it would defeat the purpose of the business. We either make it work here, in our shop, or we are done. It's binary like that.

I, for one, am glad the One Drop team found yoyos. They continue to provide a high-quality, reasonably priced "Made in America" option for yoyo makers, alongside their own line of great yoyos.

Cascadia Throws

When I got home, I told my wife, Andra, about the amazing experience. The next day, she came to me with the idea of a hipster-themed company called Cascadia Throws. The idea was to hire One Drop to make our yoyo. The company would bookend the West Coast "Hipster" world, spanning the cascades mountain range between Vancouver, Canada, and Eugene, Oregon. Thus, the Hipster Highlife was born.

We wanted to build an image that would hook the collector market — a yoyo that people were buying not just because we made a good yoyo but because they wanted to be part of the story. The name was to be a tongue-in-cheek play on the various stereotypes of "The Hipster", right down to the tagline we wanted to place on the website: "Cascadia Throws, you've probably never heard of us." We had the brand idea; now we just needed a design.

I contacted a Facebook friend and recreational yoyo designer, John Fisher, to start the process with us. He helped us get our ideas sorted out, then we handed it over to One Drop's experienced hands. I wanted the design to reference my two favorite yoyos from early in my career: the SPYY Punchline and the CLYW Chief. We nailed it. Just to give it that edge, I decided to take a concept that One Drop had played with and design the yoyo so you could attach a Lego block to it. Not only would this allow people to modify the appearance to their taste but adding even one gram of weight in different places changes the way the yoyo performs. Attaching Lego would let people make adjustments.

Anodizing Adventures

One interesting practice is the naming of individual color patterns, kind of like the swatches in a paint store. We came up with four concepts that were as "hipster" as we could get. The Foodie, The Beer Snob, The Hula Hooper, and Herb. I called Ray at MonkeyfingeR to try to convince him to do the anodizing. He didn't have time to anodize an entire batch, but he did volunteer to test some colors with us. After a dozen experiments, we had what we wanted. I contracted a well-known American company to do the actual anodizing of the full hundred yoyos.

The fine art of giving clear instructions was the skill that I clearly still hadn't mastered. I provided photos of the samples as well as detailed written instructions. The shop assured me they could match the colors. What I ended up getting was less impressive than I expected. The colors looked reasonably good, but two of the four colorways weren't what I'd asked for. One of the colors was close enough — we could still use the theme, but the other one required a branding change. For the "Hula Hooper" colorway, I had directed the anodizer to do the colors in a circular pattern around the yoyo, giving it the idea of a pile of hula hoops. This was something I knew this shop had the skills to do, and I provided a photo of the MFD sample for them to follow.

Something got missed, and I received a batch of yoyos with almost correct colors but without the ring pattern. The shop had gone the simpler route of basically splatter-painting the colors. With some adaptation and creative thinking, we made it work, and the Hula Hooper became the Starving Artist.

Unexpected Name Change

As we got the last details in place and started leaking information, a snag occurred. When Andra originally came up with the name, I googled it. The first few pages looked good. No other yoyo companies and nothing that appeared problematic, so we went with it. Once I posted our logo on Facebook for feedback, I immediately got a response pointing out a problem with the name. Cascadia is a term used to describe the bioregion including B.C., Washington, Oregon, and Northern California — an area tied together by geography, industry, and, to some degree, culture. Unfortunately, it turned out that it was also being used by an organization with racist or discriminatory overtones, which we didn't want to be involved with. Again, Andra came to the rescue with the name Rain City Skills, referencing my hometown of Vancouver in Canada. Nearly half of our days every year are rainy with an average of over 1,100 mm of rain. The name fit!

Sales — The Unboxing Experience

The packaging is what ended up setting Rain City Skills apart from other brands. Your average yoyo comes in a nice-looking box with some sort of logo on it. Inside, you'll usually find a yoyo, some string, and a sticker. I decided that if I was going to be creating something to attract collectors, I needed to do better. We pushed the hipster theme to the limit. I sourced out mason jars that would fit the yoyo and accessories. Inside you got the yoyo, custom hand-made "artisanal" string from MFD, extra Lego pieces, and a sticker all wrapped up in a hemp bag. I even had a sticker created that would fit the lid and printed a different "story" for each colorway stuck inside the lid, describing the stereotype with each hipster theme.

I contacted yoyoexpert.com and yoyosam.com, two stores that had previously carried King Yo Star yoyos. Both were excited about the package I put together. The release of the "Hipster Highlife" was very successful, considering Rain City was a brand-new company with a high-priced throw

(US$109). I sold a handful directly, and the online retail stores sold a few right away. Then we ran into an unexpected problem. A few orders arrived in broken mason jars! While mason jars are strong, they still need to be properly packaged, and no amount of packing can make up for a box getting smashed in transit. I immediately worked with the customer to solve the problem, shipping replacements for anything damaged.

The funny part is that a problem like this can be good for advertising. Yes, the customer received a less than satisfactory product, but the way we handled the situation not only resulted in a happy customer but acknowledged that my brand was safe to deal with, that we handle our problems, and put the customer first.

Collaboration as a Brand Identity

Rain City Skills has continued to grow. Our next release was the "Gamer," an unexpectedly huge success. This was a collaboration with Eternal Throw from Seattle, Washington. Free Hinton (owner of Eternal Throw) works with a charity called "Bikers Against Child Abuse." He needed a decent quality beginner yoyo to give to the kids he works with as well as one to sell at contests. I have similar needs working with yoyo clubs in schools. The idea for the Gamer was born. When I contacted Justin Scott Larson to do the design, I told him I wanted a slim, responsive yoyo that referenced the early ball-bearing yoyos of the 1990s. He came back five minutes later with a nearly complete design (which should have taken hours). He had been working on a similar idea for years.

The Gamer put Rain City on the map. I took a gamble and made five hundred of them, as that kept the price per yoyo down low enough that Free and I could afford to give away or sell them cheap to the kids we worked with. Four hundred of the yoyos were a single color, simple designs. The other hundred had complicated splash colors named after classic video games and packaged with a bunch of extra gear (bearing tool, bearing lube, pads, strings, carry case) to appeal to retail stores. What I didn't expect was that I lucked out with the timing. "Slimline" yoyos were just making a comeback and I had one priced just right. People got so excited getting all this extra gear for under fifty dollars that we ended up making two more batches of the themed color Gamers to meet demand. The combination of price and a fun theme contributed, but fortuitous timing made this a hit. At least 250-300 of the solid colors went to schools either at cost or at a loss, so this yoyo wasn't a money maker, but it did a different, more important job of putting Rain City Skills firmly on the map and in the public eye.

The Gamer really opened things up. I've continued the unboxing madness. Every throw comes with a unique package, I've even created Pokémon style trading cards for players and one for each yoyo I release! The year 2018 saw five full yoyo releases, all of which were collaborations of one sort of another. The year 2019 has been a year of madness with a release each month. I figure this will either grow the brand in a hurry or teach me some humility. I've been in awe of the great response from the community who really seems to love what we are doing. I really enjoy collaboration and try to find another brand or enthusiast to work with on every throw I release.

I've started to get a handle on this business. I've got a team of players that I can count on to help with promotion, good relationships with a couple online stores, and a variety of promotional tools at the ready. I've come a long way from the King Yo Star days! I'm slowly learning to use a variety of marketing tools (mailing lists, paid ads, giveaways) to spread awareness of the brand. When I saw a post on Facebook asking, "What's your favorite Rain City Skills yoyo," I knew I was on the right track!

PART I – SET UP YOUR BUSINESS

CHAPTER 1- BUILDING

A BRAND

The creation of a brand is a complex task with many questions to answer. Logo, name, colors, theme, story, and goals all tie in together. The first question to answer is the important one. What idea are you selling?

It's a trick question. Brands don't sell products; they sell ideas. Think about your favorite yoyo brand. What mental picture do you get? A single yoyo might come to mind, but more likely it's a logo, a sponsored player, and a look or feel. Consider what you want customers to think of when they think of your brand. Are you making high-end elite products? Low-cost fun?

Competition oriented? Artwork? Counter-culture? I'm not going to list yoyo brands, but I bet you there is a brand that comes to mind for each of those descriptors.

I have five suggestions for you to ponder — big picture ideas to help your brand to stand out in the crowd.

Novelty

Novelty is the only idea that addresses the yoyo design. Have you actually done something different? This is getting harder to do while keeping your product viable. The Rain City Skills "Loonie" stands out. It's a playable ball bearing yoyo roughly the diameter of a Canadian $1 coin. Other brands have made massively wide yoyos, just on the outside edge of being a fully functional yoyo.

Novelty can come through naming. An Australian company called Werrd made a yoyo called "Poo." The name sells the yoyo. Who doesn't want to revisit their childhood and hand a friend your yoyo and say, "Here, play with my Poo"? The brand Big Brother made "The Wedgie" and "Swirly." They had an excellent grasp on branding and novelty naming.

I've grabbed onto the "fun and creative" theme by designing yoyos outside of the competition yoyo design. The names of the throws match the theme. "The Sk8r" was shaped like a skateboard wheel. "The SETI" is shaped like a satellite dish. A yoyo called "The Ducc" doesn't really scream "competition winner," but it does get you curious. And curiosity sells products.

Personality

Your charming and well-known personality comes next. As a boutique brand owner getting started, you are the face of your brand. Down the road, you may sponsor players on your team that take over that role, but that costs money (more on that later). Some brands choose players that create videos on social media or YouTube. They engage the community through tutorials, discussions, and helpful tips. Personality is a hard one to tie a brand, but if you can do it, you will end up with a core of serious fans.

Fad

A fad is a brief but explosive popularity. You all remember the three months in 2017 when everyone and their dog had a fidget spinner? That's a fad. Fads are very difficult to predict, but if you are paying close attention to your niche market, once in a while you can catch one. I've managed to hit this correctly thrice. Once, with the King Yo Star "Rapid," again with the Rain City Skills "Gamer," and recently with the "Loonie." Each of them hit a niche that few other brands were targeting. Generally, this requires a lot of luck combined with a finger on the pulse of the market. This isn't the best basis for a business plan, but it's an important thing to be aware of.

Flare

By flare, I'm referring to everything except the actual yoyo. It's easy to put a yoyo in a box with a string and try to sell it. But can you add something extra to make people feel like they are getting a deal? I've seen everything from candy to a branded campfire-style aluminum coffee mug. I recall one brand that released a yoyo in a complex metal box that cost almost as much as the yoyo to make! An unusual type of finish to add (gold plating?) or a custom handmade string and carry bag combo is an easy option for adding value.

With Rain City Skills, I tend to go over the top, but that has worked for me. People buy my yoyos, in part, because of the unboxing experience. They know they are going to get a yoyo surrounded by accessories, decorations, and unique packaging. Collectors especially love this sort of thing, but really it appeals to all of us. Who doesn't want to feel like they got more than their money's worth? You need to figure out what feels authentic to you.

Story

The human brain is made for stories. It's how we organize our memories. I once attended a teaching workshop where the presenter asked the following question: "If I showed you a list of thirty words for ten seconds, how many could you remember?" I stuck my hand up and replied: "Three." The presenter then told a story, using each of the words on the list. It was a nonsense story, but by the end, I could remember twenty of the thirty words.

If you can make your brand and your product part of a story, people will remember. I don't mean you have to write a novel (although that could be a fun marketing trick), but give your yoyo a character. When I released the Rain City "Gamer," each colorway had a specific video game theme. People bought specific colors because the game was a part of their personal story. I know of one brand that creates yoyos based around mythical nautical creatures. Another, around the game of chess. Just having a naming theme isn't enough. Image your yoyo is a character in a comic book series. What is its origin story? Superpower? Weaknesses? When we talk later about selling yoyos to a retail store, this is a key feature. Retail store owners know that stories sell yoyos.

NAME

Your first and arguably most important decision is a name. Your brand name needs to do one of two things:

1. Tell your customers directlsy what you sell — "Duckhat Yoyos."
2. Create an emotional or intellectual connection to the product and your story — " Science Toys for Engineering Magic."

Brainstorm some solid ideas and roll them around your head for a while. Start developing your first release and really think about your story and how the name lines up. You can read blogs until your eyes bleed looking at lists of tips for naming (I did while preparing this), but I'll save you a bit of time.

Easy to say, Easy to remember

Your name is how customers find you, remember you, and recommend you to their friends. Imagine a conversation with someone on the street.

"Hey, what's that you are playing with?"
"It's a yoyo!"
"Cool, where do I get one?"
"Just head to my website, rotationalgravitydicombobulationdevices.com"

What are the odds your potential customer is going to remember your site? They will probably end up on Amazon, buying the first thing that comes up with a search for "yoyo." Make your name something that rolls off the tongue and is easy for customers to remember — either with a short name or a good acronym.

Acronym

An acronym is what you get when you take the initial letters of a series of words and say it as a word. For example, National Aeronautics and Space Administration — NASA, or Computer-Aided Design — CAD. Both examples create a collection of letters that are pronounced as a word. Alternatively, you have an "Initialism," which is when the initial letters are pronounced separately, like CIA (Central Intelligence Agency). You say each letter separately.

A short, single-syllable brand name is easy to remember but will limit its organic reach in the beginning. Unless you know the story of a brand called "Noince," the word itself is meaningless.

A short phrase will tell people what you are selling but will get shortened to an acronym by customers. So plan for that. A great example is the Canadian brand "Saturn Precision Yoyos." The name tells you exactly what they sell, and their acronym is a single syllable that is memorable and sounds cool. That was one thing I didn't think about when creating Rain City Skills. While the words roll off the tongue nicely, RCS doesn't make an acronym, and the three letters don't roll of the tongue as an initialism. (Say it out loud.) Serious People in Nations isn't great for advertising yoyos, but you get the fantastic acronym: SPIN! Generate some names, record yourself saying them out loud, and have a discussion about imaginary yoyos by your brand with a friend.

LOGO

A logo goes hand in hand with a name. It is what people see first when they click on your social media. It's at the top of your email and website headers and is what shops and reviewers use to identify you. I can't stress enough how important it is to hire a professional. Even if you have mad photoshop skills, logo design is a separate skill set.

Consider what your logo says. What does it advertise? The Rain City Skills logo isn't perfect. It's an outline of the Vancouver city skyline. What I didn't consider is that Seattle is also a rainy city with a space needle in the middle of its skyline. I might have been better off with a simpler logo, but once you've started marketing with a logo it's a challenge to switch it up.

Image or words? Consider what it's going to look like in a thumbnail on your Instagram profile or on a stage banner at a contest. When I started the Boutique Yoyo Collective, our first logo told people where to go to find out more about us. It was great on a sticker or business card. But it was unintelligible on a stage banner. We had a different designer have a go at it, and they came up with simpler design.

Trademark and Similar Products

You want a great name, but you don't want to be too similar to another yoyo brand. I ran into this problem years ago when I was representing King Yo Star. A small store owner in Texas had purchased a trademark on his own brand called Yoyo King and objected to my using a brand name that was similar. He wanted me to either stop using the name or license my brand name from him. I looked into the rules and established that King Yo Star had been selling yoyos in the USA before Yoyo King, which gave my claim some precedence. Instead of fighting him, I purchased a trademark on the name. He could have pursued it, but at that point, it wouldn't have been worth the legal battle. Check out the patent and trademark listing in your country and any other country where you plan to do business. It's worth it to buy your trademark if you are planning on building a long-term business.

Brand Colors

Color matters. If you have a consistent color theme throughout your branding, it makes for better brand recognition. If you can match colors across social media, photos, and print goods, it's easier for your customers to recognize your brand.

Start by looking at your website (more on how to set that up in a bit). Search through templates and find one that resonates with you. It'll have a pre-set color scheme. Make a sample website, share it with some yoyoers, and ask their opinion. Then talk to your designer and tie in your logo colors.

DOMAIN NAME AND SEO

Domain name refers to your website address. When we get into setting up a website, I'll go more into how to set that up. You can use any domain name sites to search through available names. You want to make sure your website can be either your name or your acronym (buy both if you can).

Make sure you search up your brand name on a domain registrar early in your process. You don't want to find out after you've paid for a logo that your website isn't available. You also don't want to choose a domain name that is too similar to others. If I actually wanted to start the fictitious brand Duckhat Yoyos, my first problem would be that duckhat.com is taken. I'd have to use duckhatyoyos.com and risk confusing customers typing in the first address.

SEO stands for search engine optimization. This is a form of modern-day sorcery that I only partially understand. It deals with how search engines find and list websites. What happens when you search your potential brand name on search engines or social media? I discarded one potential brand name because the first page of a google search brought up a politically troubling organization. I didn't want that association with my brand. Conversely, if you choose a name that has too many other results, it's going to be hard for potential customers to see it. Anything starting with "yoyo" is going to have a fair bit of competition. If you wanted your brand to be "Yoyo Monster," there are multiple different yoyos with the word "monster" in the name. Take the time to search up your potential name everywhere and think hard about the competition. If you choose to run paid ads down the road, your search terms get more expensive if there is more competition.

SOCIAL MEDIA AND EMAIL ACCOUNTS

Part of your naming process is determining what will work/is available on social media. Look at the platforms that you are most likely to be on. What comes up with your search? If there are numerous similar names, consider something different. If your brand name is already in use on one platform, that is going to be a problem. Either you are going to grow and want control of it, or you might be looking at legal issues with trademark down the road.

The simplest thing to do when getting started would be to use your personal account (Gmail/Outlook/Yahoo, etc.). Don't do that. At the very least, start a second email account for your business. It looks a little more professional and gives you a layer of separation between your personal presence on the Internet and that of your brand.

The free option is to simply set up a new email account with one of the various services like Gmail. If you work with google drive, it will make your life easier to have all your files in one place.

Long-term, you will want a custom email address linked to your website. Instead of an email address like "duckhat@gmail.com," you get "info@duckhat.com." Your brand name becomes the "@" location. Your registrar likely offers a service for a monthly fee. You also have the paid option on sites like Wix and Squarespace to setup a private mail through Google's "Gsuite." It's up to you to decide what that extra touch of professionalism is worth to you, but it's there as an option.

The process of creating and building up a brand can devour your life. The key when you start is to get the basics in place and to be consistent. Don't get intimidated by how much there is to do. You can start small and build up the skills you need to expand your brand.

CHAPTER 2 – RUNNING

A BUSINESS

Paperwork. Everyone hates it. Keep on top of it, and you'll avoid the biggest mistake you can make. Make a plan, set up your structure from the beginning, and save yourself a mountain of headache later.

No matter how small your business is, there are rules, laws, and taxes to take care of. None of these are too complex, but if you don't get organized from the start, you'll run into trouble when you scale up later. This section is here to provide you with some suggested starting points. I also outline some good practices for keeping yourself organized as you move forward with your business.

One topic that is well beyond the scope of this book is financial management. I'm not going to tackle that beyond recommending that if you don't have a grip on our personal finances, get some advice on that first. Then talk to someone about planning how you will manage your money as a business. Regular record keeping and review of your finances is critical if you are going to make this a success, or at the very least keep it fun. It's really easy to find yourself nickel and dimed to death by monthly subscription fees, user fees, and credit card interest if you don't have a plan. Schedule-in time each month to keep on top of the money.

What follows is not legal advice. I am neither a lawyer nor an accountant, and I absolutely recommend consulting both of these as needed. Please do your research to ensure you follow the laws and regulations where you do business.

BUSINESS LOCATION AND LICENSE

If this is your first time going into business for yourself, you need to spend some time learning the rules. These rules differ depending on where you live. This section is not exhaustive but introduces some of the puzzle pieces.

Laws vary. So do license and tax regulations for small business. Your business will need an official location (most likely your house). You will most likely need to apply for a business license in your city. Most governments require you to register to get a tax code of some sort. This usually goes along with submitting quarterly or annual tax statements. For example: In British Columbia, Canada, you don't have to register for a Federal GST number (Goods and Services Tax) until you have earned more than $30,000 over four or less consecutive quarters. In the province of British Columbia, you do need to collect Provincial Sales Tax right from your first sale. For more information, visit the Government of Canada webpage.

There are benefits to running an official business. A small business accountant can advise you on how best to manage deductions and write-offs. If you travel to contests, your costs can be set against profits. Do you run your business out of your home? Part of your rent or mortgage may also be a business cost. Keep in mind that your home insurance will need to be changed to accommodate a home business. A regular home insurance plan won't cover the space used for your office or your inventory and equipment.

If you want to sell on Amazon, you need to be able to provide a tax number as well as a trademark for your business. You may run into other situations where having that legally recognized presence is critical.

When you first start out, you're probably going to be running a type of business called a "sole proprietorship." This means your business is part of you and not a separate corporation. It also means you're going to do some things differently when you file your tax returns. Other options for creating a business vary depending on where you live. Your country and province/state will likely have guides on their official website to help you make the right choice. A small business accountant will be able to help you get organized, so you are ready come tax time. It is your responsibility to make sure you are following the law.

TAXES

A good investment at the beginning of your business setup is to spend some time with an accountant. If you plan your methods of collecting information right from the start, your life will be a lot easier come tax time. Don't do what I did and get to the end of your first year with a notebook full of chicken scratch and no receipts to submit. I ended up paying far more taxes that year than I should have because I did not have an effective accounting system in place.

In the beginning, you can get away with using a basic spreadsheet, although that's not the best option. The better choice is to learn basic accounting software from the beginning. If you don't use an accountant from the start, at least make sure you know what can and can't be claimed on your taxes. Get ahold of the tax form for a small business and base your accounting on that.

Keep receipts. All of them. For everything you do related to the business in any way. Your local tax law may allow for things like food consumed during business meetings. For example, the costs I incur when I travel to yoyo contests to promote and sell the brand are a tax deduction where I do business. But only if I have receipts; a bank or credit card statement isn't good enough.

Examples of things that MAY be deductible (consult your local tax laws):

- cell phone if used for business
- computer and software
- desk, shelving, storage, printer paper, packaging materials
- your car (track mileage when using it to travel to the post office or yoyo club meets)
- your mortgage/rent/utilities (If you are using a room in your home as a dedicated office, you may be able to write off a portion of your costs.)
- any product given away for sponsorship, marketing, or customer retention
- licenses
- educational training (business courses, online classes, and business books, including this one!)

Strategies for managing your receipts and invoices:

- Write notes on the receipt, explaining why it's a business expense.
- Get a wallet with two sections for bills and keep receipts in one of them.
- Take a photo with your cell phone camera, ideally with Google Drive's scan feature or with a receipt scanner app.
- Print invoices immediately and store them in a folder in your email, Dropbox or Google Drive for quick reference. I have a wireless printer at home, and I am able to email things to it to print. When I'm on the bus and pay an invoice on my phone, I send the invoice to print right away.

- Don't be afraid to pay someone to keep on top of your paperwork. If you are like me, it'll pile up and be a disaster. A small amount of money to hire an underemployed friend once a month to do some filing can save you a headache at tax time.

If you want to reduce your paperwork hassle each month, look into the variety of receipt management apps available. You want to find one that will scan the receipt and pull out the date, address, name of the place, and the taxes. I use one called Veryfi, which collects that info and then generates a spreadsheet each month.

BANK ACCOUNT AND CREDIT CARD

Open a second bank account. Go to your bank and tell them you want a business account. Don't let them talk you into a bunch of unnecessary services. This should be free to begin with. Shop around to see what different financial institutions can offer you. They will be motivated to get your business, so take advantage of that.

It's a lot easier to manage your incoming payments and keep track of your money if it's separate from your personal account. It'll also allow you to set up a separate PayPal account for your business.

You may choose to sign up for a business credit card. This can be a useful tool if you find one with a good points program. My points generally cover two-three flights to yoyo contests per year. Use caution and restraint though. A credit card is the most expensive way to borrow money. Get one only if you have the discipline to make sure that it is always paid off on time. Paying interest more than offsets any benefits from collecting points. When I started, I carried a balance on my credit card for a year and paid more in interest than I earned in points. Now I use the business credit card constantly, but I pay it off as soon as I use it.

Financing a business is a topic for another book. But I will say you are better off looking into a bank loan or saving for a while before starting. Crowdfunding is a relatively new way to finance a business. Sites like GoFundMe and Kickstarter offer an organized and official solution. They also have fees to budget for. You can also crowdfund directly using PayPal or through your webstore service. If you don't have anything unique to offer, or a big name behind you, crowdfunding will be difficult. You also run the risk of alienating customers before they even buy anything. The first experience anyone has of your brand should not be a request for money. That can be off-putting. Most yoyo shoppers are used to buying products that are made and ready to go.

DIGITAL STORAGE AND ORGANIZATION

When you set up your brand, you likely chose an email service. If you opted for Outlook or Gmail, you have access to their cloud storage. If not, Dropbox is a good alternative. No matter your choice, you want access to cloud-based storage for your logos, product photos, and other files.

If you are anything like me, you're constantly bouncing between multiple devices. Files on my various devices are a mess, but what I put in Google Drive is easy to find and is accessible from anywhere.

Organization is very important, and since I use Google Drive, that's what I'm going to talk about here. Start up by giving yourself a few different folders: logos, videos, promo pics, receipts, accounting, sponsorship, contacts.

Keep track of contact information of people whom you have worked with or may want to work with. A spreadsheet works fine. Networking is an important part of your business, and you never know when you are going to need to borrow or hire a set of skills.

Google Drive has a variety of built-in tools. The spreadsheet and document editor are the most obvious, but the forms are a very underrated tool. I often use Google forms to collect information. You can create a series of questions ranging from multiple choice to paragraph answer. It also pulls the answers together in a graph or a spreadsheet. I designed the Rain City Skills "The DUCC" yoyo through a series of surveys using forms (more on this later). Forms also allow you to collect uploaded files so you can have people submit a picture or a video as part of a contest. Just be aware of your data storage limits. You can upgrade for a rather small annual fee if you come close to your limit.

INVENTORY MANAGEMENT

Keeping accurate records of your inventory is critical. If you know what you have sold and what you have in stock, you can calculate profit. The amount of extra work required to track this information depends on what you use to sell your product. If you wholesale to a retail store exclusively, keeping track is easy. Odds are you'll use PayPal and if you generate your invoices directly in PayPal, all your accounting is right there. If you sell directly through Facebook, you have to record each sale yourself.

The easiest solution is to use a website service with a built-in e-commerce system. Use it to create a report of your sales, and the information is all there. I'm really scatterbrained, and I can't count on remembering to record things, so I try to make sure everything goes through my store. This has the added bonus of making sure I don't forget to ship on time. It also helps at tax time. You still need to do a full inventory count to double-check, but good records help you calculate your taxes owed.

SHIPPING

Shipping is the most critical part of online sales. Shipping fees are a barrier to purchase. The higher the fee, the higher the chance a customer will abandon their order. Likewise, a three-week transit time. Your average customer wants fast and either cheap or free. You will want to charge enough to cover the actual shipping costs as well as your time, in packaging.

Problem #1 – Cost

In a perfect world, your shipping rate would include the following:

- purchasing postage and insurance
- cost of office supplies related to shipping (box, tape, etc.)
- cost of labor involved in shipping

The reality is that shipping is an area where you're likely to take a loss. You often compete with other online retailers offering lower rates that you can't match. Your product may be unique and can't be purchased elsewhere, but you also compete against hundreds of other "unique" yoyo providers.

Perception is the key. Amazon's Prime program is as successful as it is because it gives you fast delivery and the illusion of free shipping. I say *illusion* because you can often find comparable products that aren't fulfilled by Amazon and that are priced lower. I know I'll still pay more for the faster shipping. Obviously, you aren't competing with Amazon, but keep in mind how much you hate waiting for a package. If you charge $65 for your newest yoyo plus $15 for shipping, a customer may choose a different brand whose shipping charge is only $5 or nothing at all.

I know I don't get many sales from outside of North America because I charge a high international shipping rate. The rate reflects the variability depending on destination and package size, as well as the complexities of tracking overseas. I could offer a significantly lower-priced option with no tracking, but then I'm on the hook for lost packages, which gets expensive and time consuming. At this point it's not worth the few added sales for me, but down the road I might make the change if the demand is there.

If you sell direct, you have the flexibility of building shipping into your price so you can give your customers that same illusion. Of course, that's going to depend on where the customers are and what shipping costs are like where you live. In the U.S., a single yoyo costs about $5 to ship. If you ship into Canada, you need to look at about $20.

Problem #2 – Time

How long are you willing to wait for a new yoyo? If it's a good enough deal, I'll wait for a month, but if I'm comparison shopping, I'll choose the option with the fastest shipping speed.

When I started, I was using Canada Post and was shipping out whenever I could fit in a trip to the post office after work. This meant my Canadian customers were often waiting for three to five days for the product to be shipped. My customers outside of Canada were waiting for two to three weeks to receive the product. On top of that, it cost US$15–$20.

A friend pointed me to a service that changed my business and tripled my sales overnight. Now, I drop off my packages, and the company then drives them across the border into the United States, where they are handed off to the U.S. Postal Service ("USPS"). The transit time is now two to three days, and my cost is US$5–$6.

Problem #3 – Postal Service

Your country's post office may or may not be your most effective option. In Canada, it's pretty much the only viable option that doesn't break the bank. In the United States, the postal service is a pretty solid and consistent system protected by law. Having said that, your location might make a courier service (DHL, FedEx, etc.) a better option.

Part of the process of setting up your website is looking at shipping integrations. I chose Shopify because the cross-border service I use integrates with Shopify. This means postage is automatically created when a customer places an order, so I don't spend hours manually creating labels. Depending on your region, your website platform might offer bulk shipping prices. You might also find a third-party service that does so.

Packaging is a key component of keeping your costs down. The service I use offers cubic discount rates. That means if I use boxes with the right dimensions, I get a discount. I know USPS offers flat rate boxes, but you also might be better off purchasing in bulk from a packaging supplier such as Uline.

Starting a business is a complicated task, at least if you want to do it right. Forethought and planning save time and money down the road, so it's worth taking some time at the beginning. Accounting and taxes, licensing, banking, inventory, and shipping management are far from the fun parts of making yoyos. If you want to keep making yoyos though, you need to get on top of all of these aspects of business. Once you have the big picture of your brand planned out, it's time to start building the customer experience. We'll begin with a website.

CHAPTER 3 - WEBSITE

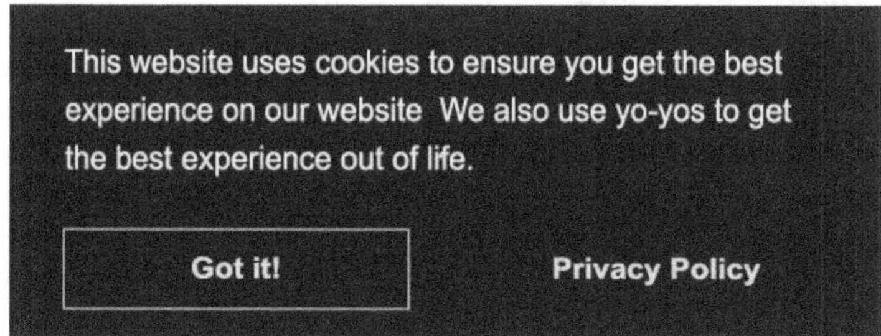

Keywords:

Domain name or *URL* — your address www.somethingsomething.com
Registrar — where you go to buy your domain name
Web hosting — where your actual website information lives. This is different from the domain name.
Website builder — a service that allows you to build a website, often combined with webhosting
Integrations — apps that build themselves into your website. Can be either created by the website builder or a third party and may be free, paid, or subscription based.

A website is critical for a modern business of any sort, particularly one that exists online. It is possible to run a yoyo brand without one, but you miss out on a lot of marketing opportunities. Not to fear, getting a website is actually a very easy process now.

When I was in university, I built a website. This is back in ancient times. The teacher education program was in the middle of changes and was allowing digital teaching portfolios instead of physical scrapbook-style final projects. A handful of us built websites (that never made it onto the Internet). It was a nightmare of a learning curve with a very complex interface where every detail had to be manually created. I finished it, but it took dozens of hours of frustration.

Twelve years later, a beginner can set up a far more attractive and complex website in about twenty minutes. A variety of services exist specifically to make building and running a website as simple as possible. This means that you can build and maintain a professional-looking website with relative ease. You will use it to talk about your brand, introduce yourself and your team, display and sell products, and share news and updates.

If this isn't something you are comfortable doing, you also have the option of outsourcing this work. There is no shortage of people who build websites for a living. Keep in mind that you still have to provide the content to make design decisions. The Rain City Skills website is one I built myself. I hired someone to build the Mryoyothrower website because I didn't have the time to do it myself. Of course, this comes with a cost, but you may be able to barter. There are plenty of tech-savvy people in the yoyo community, who might be willing to help you set up your website and maintain it in exchange for yoyos.

Before you launch your website, you do want to have your branding organized — your company name, logo, and domain name. If you haven't purchased your domain name, go grab it now! Once you are ready, have a look at one or more of the options I cover in this chapter.

BUILDING AND HOSTING YOUR WEBSITE

Domain Name

First step is to head to a registrar like Namecheap or Sibername. These sites allow you to register a domain name for an annual fee, usually around US$10. This can also be done through the website services listed in the next section, but I recommend owning your domain name yourself. This gives you the option of switching website services later with minimal hassle.

Using a site like Namecheap also gives you the easy option of multiple URLs. I have both www.raincityskills.com and www.raincityskills.ca pointed to my website. This way, I increase my website's visibility and make it easier for customers to find it, using Google search. I've also got www.returntopshop.com pointing there, so any of my old customers or links to Return Top Shop will still point to my website.

Build and Host

Web hosting is a semi-complicated subject. Your web host is where the website exists. It has to sit on physical computer servers somewhere. A myriad of services exists for simple hosting. If you opt to learn how to use WordPress, you can host your website wherever you want. This can be both the least expensive and the most powerful website-building option. It's also the most complicated to get started with, which is why I recommend a full-service website builder if you are already intimidated by the idea of building a website yourself or simply don't want to spend the time.

A website service is different from hosting. Weebly, Shopify, Squarespace, and Wix are examples of website builder services that also offer web hosting as part of their package. These sites have built-in tools to help get your website up and running. They offer built-in systems for running an online store, marketing, and shipping. The following section outlines the five services listed above, starting with easy and working up to complex.

At time of writing, I have websites hosted through Weebly (www.canadayoyo.ca), Shopify (www.raincityskills.com), Squarespace (www.mryoyothrower.com), and Wix (jdmckay.com). I attempted WordPress on multiple occasions, but each time, I decided that the learning curve and frustration weren't worth the effort. I do know many people who use it very successfully. I'm not going to get into an exhaustive comparison of the options. You can find up-to-date comparison charts easily online. I explain below why I chose each web host and what I've noticed about them.

Weebly

My first website was with Weebly. I chose it at random years ago for my classroom blog. I've since used it for a number of websites. It hosts the Canadian Yoyo Association website as well as the website for my Grade 1/2 class. It's a good starting point if you've never built website, as it's simple to learn and affordable. The free package gives you time to learn how to use it. The free options don't allow you to connect your domain name, so you will need to upgrade to basic paid package when you are ready to go public. A more expensive e-commerce package will be necessary for direct sales.

Wix

I've recently started using Wix for my author page. I chose it because, like Weebly, it has a free option and a US$5 per month option to link your own domain. I find the editor more complicated to manage than Weebly. It's taking some getting used to, but the basic functions are easy. I will warn you that their sales tactics are aggressive. Don't make the mistake I did and accept the "Limited time 50 per cent off a one-year subscription" deal at face value and jump before you are ready. If my experience is common, you will likely keep getting that email for months until you are ready to upgrade.

Squarespace

I use Squarespace for the Mryoyothrower website. I started out on Weebly but got frustrated with the iPad app. I found that it crashed frequently while I was writing blogs. This was a few years ago, and I'm sure it's improved, but it prompted me to try Squarespace. I hired a professional to build the site and transfer the content because I was too busy to do it myself. It ended up looking great and I'm glad I made the change. Hiring a pro to set it up allowed me to learn the platform at my leisure to make changes.

I haven't fully explored the platform, but my understanding is that Squarespace has a more powerful editing tool than Weebly or Wix. It's also a little more difficult to find your way around, but only marginally. It does not offer a free plan, but it does offer a 14-day free trial. One benefit is that their e-commerce package is reasonably priced. The blog setup works well for me, which was main purpose for switching to Squarespace.

Shopify

When I was running Return Top Shop, I started out with Weebly. I actually put the store together in a weekend of flurried activity. I'm the type of person who when having an idea has to either do it right there and then or not at all. So rather than look into the best option, I went with what I already knew.

Eventually, that turned out to be a mistake, as I hit the limit of Weebly's functionality as an e-commerce platform.

At that point, I shopped around and made the decision to move to Shopify. Shopify is an e-commerce platform first, so it worked better for running a complex retail business. When I shut down Return Top Shop, I switched the Rain City Skills website over to my Shopify account. I'd previously been handling Rain City sales through Return Top Shop, so it made sense to keep the inventory in one place.

The biggest reason though was Shopify's third-party shipping service integrations. I can connect the special cross-border shipping program I use, to the website. Shopify sends orders to my shipping software, and I don't have to type all the information in. If you are in the U.S., this is less of a deciding point, as the other options also offer bulk or discounted shipping services built in. Shopify is probably the most complicated of the options short of WordPress. My biggest complaint is that your ability to create and edit non-product pages is very limited without a paid third-party app installed. So non-product pages like my team page don't look as good as I'd like it to.

It's also the most expensive of the three options, although only by a few dollars. You can connect your eBay and Amazon seller account, so all your inventory is tracked in one place. The Shopify app store also offers great third-party options for just about anything you want your website to do. I run a points program on raincityskills.com (it pops up after 5 seconds on the site) where you get points per dollar spent that convert to discounts.

I've seen other sites use add-ons like a spin wheel that pops up and offers a deal or discount. Be wary, every time something pops up, you run the risk of irritating your shopper. Make sure if you use one of these options, you have it set to a time delay (so it's not a barrier to entry right away), and you have only one.

I hesitate to recommend Shopify to a new brand getting started, as it's probably more than you need, but it's worth a look if you are planning on growing your brand beyond a couple releases a year.

WordPress

I will start with a disclaimer I have fought with WordPress repeatedly over the years to no avail. I've read that it's the most powerful and flexible website creation tool on the market. Squarespace, Wix and Weebly are user-friendly, but user-friendly comes with limitations. If you know what you are doing WordPress can be built for any purpose and can be beautiful and highly functional. If you know what you are doing. The learning curve getting started is higher than the other options, but the cost is lower. Wordpress.org is free to build with if you provide hosting. You download the software to build your website for free, then upload it to the webhost. Namecheap offers hosting service. This is your cheapest option getting started (hosting can be as low as $2 or $3). This one is the best option if you are looking to learn more about web design and have the widest range of options long term. It's also an option if you are looking to hire a professional to manage your website.

WEBSITE CONTENT

The most important advice I can offer when the time comes to add content to your website is to edit everything before publishing. Then edit it again. Then get a friend to proofread it. Write your content in a word processor and spellcheck it before uploading. Use a grammar editor like Hemmingway App (free browser-based program) to simplify your writing. Record yourself reading your content aloud and listen to it or use a text-to-voice program to read it to you. Grammatical errors put people off. If you can't get your advertising copy correct, what have you missed in your yoyo design?

Here are a few pages to include:
- Welcome
- Product or Store
- Team — if you have sponsored players
- About/Contact/Privacy Policy
- Blog

You want a **Welcome** page. Keep this as clean and simple as you can. Have your logo, some sort of product gallery, and your mailing list sign-up form (more on this later). You need a page for your products. Some companies just use a store page (I do); others also include separate page, listing all the products they have made. The second option is a good way to help new fans see what you have done in the past.

You'll also need a page to showcase your **team** if you choose to sponsor players. This page usually showcases photos, a couple videos, and a biography. This content should match your theme. If you sell high-end competitive yoyos, include serious biographies with well-edited videos or competition videos. If you sell to the "fun and silly" market, the biographies can read like Terry Pratchett wrote them.

An **About, Contact**, and **Privacy Policy** are also a good idea. The bottom of most websites is where this information is usually stored, along with links to all your social media.

Don't clutter up your website with too many pages, images, and too much information. Make it easy for customers to see what you make and how to buy it. Make sure your images are of professional quality and clear. Hire someone to run them through Photoshop if you lack those skills.

While you edit, double-check that it looks good on mobile as well as the browser. Half of your potential customers shop on their smartphones these days. I know that if I go to a website and everything gets tiny or jumbled, I don't stay long. The website builder platforms listed above are pretty good at adapting your site for both mobile and browser - but always double-check your content on both.

Blog

A blog is a great tool for communicating new releases, running contests, and offering added value to draw customers to your website. Mix up your promo posts with regular posts sharing useful content. "Hey, check out this great blog post about the contest I attended!" will get your social media posts more clicks than "Hey check out my website and buy my yoyos!" Here are a few format suggestions for blog posts to keep it easy to add them:

- three tutorial videos you've learned something from recently

- sharing a trick video you watched, adding some commentary
- tips and tricks (Did you know...)
- trick videos that are worth watching
- personal stories that relate to yoyo (Yesterday, this person saw me yoyo at the bus stop...)
- non-yoyo related posts that you tie into yoyos (my sibling had their first baby last week! I can't wait to teach my new niece how to yoyo.)
- talking about other brand's yoyos.

This last one is a bit counter-intuitive, but cross-promotion is useful. Talk to other small brands and exchange blog posts. You write about their yoyo; they write about yours. Or talk about yoyos that have inspired your designs, elements of that design that really work for you.

If you decide to use a blog as a marketing tool, just remember to keep it updated, even with simple promo posts. If I'm looking around for a website and the last blog post was in 2012, I'm going to wonder how current the brand is and whether it's safe to buy a yoyo from them. This could be a task for a sponsored player - they could provide you with a short article a few times a month. If you don't have the time to do this, hold off on the blog and focus your attention where it'll do the most good. Don't spread yourself too thin.

At the end of the day, you need to consider your ability level and free time, as well as the possible growth of your business. I spent nearly $800 moving my Return Top Shop website from Weebly to Shopify because I didn't plan for growth. It was 100 per cent worth it, but if I had been planning for growth from the beginning, I would have made different choices at the start.

At the end of the day, your choice for a website depends on your skill:

1. Limited web building and computer skills — Weebly or Wix
2. Reasonable computer skills and some web building experience — Squarespace
3. Either experience or time to learn — Shopify or WordPress

As well as your goals and needs

1. Boutique brand making one-two yoyos per year — Weebly, Wix, or Squarespace
2. Boutique brand intending to grow fast - Shopify or WordPress

There is no downside to trying each of them to see what works for you. The most important part is that you are able to update the site with ease to keep the content fresh and keep viewers engaged with your content.

Key Takeaway Thoughts

1. Buy your domain name right now, even if you aren't going to set up the website. I use Namecheap; you should explore the options to choose the right service for you.
2. Choose a website service that meets your needs and matches your ability/time level. Don't be afraid to try a few before deciding. Some options are: Weebly, Wix, Squarespace, Shopify, WordPress.
3. Keep your website simple and clean, make it easy to shop with high-quality, clean photos.

4. Edit all of your writing, have a friend double-check it.
5. If you choose to use a blog, keep it updated!

Building and maintaining a website can be a fair bit of work, but it's really only as difficult as you want it to be. If this task is outside of your skill set or desire to learn, consider hiring out, either paying a professional or trading a couple of yoyos to someone with the skills.

PART II - MARKETING

J.D. McKay

52

CHAPTER 4 - CONTENT CREATION

Keywords

Marketing — The art of (1) finding people who don't know that they need what your brand offers and (2) subtly nudging them towards the decision to buy

Advertising — A direct message asking someone to take action (purchase, click, read, etc)
Copy writing — Writing that is explicitly intended to sell products
Content writing — Writing that offers value to potential customers to engage interest
Call to action — Any content that asks viewers to take an action in response (for example, a simple question, a poll or a survey, or a request for comment)
Organic reach — The number of people your posted content will get to without the use of paid ads
Onboarding sequence — A series of automated emails that welcome new subscribers

Marketing involves science, art, research and a fair bit of luck. It requires both short-term actions and long-term planning. It is also a lot of work.

If you are trying to build a viable brand, everything you do needs to feed into the question of "Why are people going to buy my brand?" The answer isn't as simple as you think. Making a good yoyo isn't enough. "long spinning," "well balanced," "smooth playing," "championship quality" describe almost all the yoyos on the market. How does yours stand out beyond these descriptors?

The process of advertising isn't a blunt instrument. We've all suffered from spam emails, repetitive cries of "buy my yoyo, it's awesome", and other heavy-handed sales tactics. These leave us feeling distrust and disinterest more often than not. To avoid becoming one of these brands, you must carefully curate your presence in the online world. Balance your marketing with a blend of techniques.

Here are a couple overarching strategies to keep in mind as we move forward.

The Gentle Touch

One idea I see a lot is called "The Seven Touches of Marketing" or "The Rule of 7." This refers to the number of times, on average, you need to "touch" or make contact with a potential customer before they will buy your product. People don't usually buy from an unknown brand the first time they see it. We all work hard for our money and hesitate to gamble with it. Trust sells product, and there are a number of ways to earn that trust. References, reviews, or just repeated exposure can get you there.

Consider this: you have enough money to go to one restaurant this month, and it has to be one you haven't eaten at. Are you more likely to go to the one you've at least seen a few times before, or the one you've never heard of? "I drive by that place every day" is an irrational but common reason to choose a place to shop. You need to put yourself on your customer's digital drive to work.

Trust in a brand sells product, and it usually takes a few encounters to cross over from "strange new thing, fear it" to "familiar safe thing, I'll buy it." Big corporations can't be sure how many sales are generated by the dollars spent on billboard signs, but I guarantee you that if they stopped buying that space, sales would drop. Marketing gently guides your potential customers to the point where they start trusting your brand. Then, when you advertise directly with that "buy my awesome yoyo" post, it's met with excitement instead of irritation.

The 80:20 Rule

Another really solid piece of advice I keep running across is that your interactions with the online world should be about *80 per cent* give, *20 per cent* ask. This is one of the most important concepts to keep in mind as you navigate the online world. No one likes advertising being shoved in their face. The majority of what you do should be adding value to the community you are marketing to, earning you the right to directly advertise some of the time. I'll cover a variety of options to help you with this. Sponsoring players and contests, giveaways, free content, helpful advice and volunteering your time are all great examples of ways to add value.

The following section will outline options for marketing your product. Don't feel like you need to master everything at once. It's better to put quality effort into one or two things than to be inconsistent in many.

The volume of content that crosses a social media feed each day is enormous. If you are to have any chance of crossing the path of new customers, you will need content and a lot of it. In this chapter, I will guide you through writing content and using photos and videos for your marketing. We'll begin with some general tips on writing, photography, and video. After that, I'll dive into a selection of social media sites and revisit the best use for each of these content formats.

WRITING

Video and audio are critically important in advertising, but crafting the written word is still an essential skill. Once your image or video has drawn a potential customer in, the writing is what closes the deal. I'm going to cover two different types of writing in this chapter: *content writing* and *copywriting*.

Content writing offers something of use to the customer — a story, a guide, or an editorial on a topic that nudges customers to action instead of directing them. This book is a prime example. I've created a guide that potential new customers will read. I'm not advertising directly; instead, I trust that readers who enjoy this book will be curious about the author.

Copywriting calls the reader to action — usually, the purchase of a good or service. It is persuasive writing in clear and succinct chunks. You don't list attributes and tell stories; you use carefully crafted phrases to evoke an emotional response.

Writing advertising is a skill different from most other types of writing you may have done. I'm far from an expert on the subject, but I'm learning. The biggest thing is to give your readers the most information you can, using the smallest number of easy-to-read words. A short essay on the features of your new release is far less likely to get read than a simple list of bullet points. There is a reason why brands hire advertising experts to come up with simple slogans like "Eat Fresh" and "Taste the Rainbow." If you can associate a short, catchy phrase with your brand, you are able to advertise more widely with less effort.

A product description is a direct advertisement. That means you need to give the customer (1) enough information to make the choice to buy but (2) not so much they lose interest. Here are three variations on a fictitious product description:

Option #1

The newest release from Canadian Yoyo Brand Duckhat called "The Hat-Hat" is now available. This is a yoyo that has many amazing features, such as a ball bearing that is U-shaped to keep the string centered. It also features a cup designed for executing tricks with the yoyo balanced on the tip of one's finger a.k.a. "fingerspin" tricks. The yoyo is available in three different colors that were very carefully planned out. The first one is blue — similar to the color of the sky, where ducks love to soar. The second one is red — similar to that of a rose. The third one is black, similar to the heart of anyone who doesn't think ducklings are adorable little balls of snuggly fluff. You can purchase yours from a variety of yoyo stores on the Internet, such as Louisiana's own Fowl Yoyo's, the hottest little shop on the corner of Bob Street and Doug Way in Toronto, Indignant Return Tops, and more!

Option #2

The "Hat-Hat" from Duckhat Yoyos has a U-shaped ball bearing, fingerspin cup and three great colors: sky-blue, rose-red, and puppy-hater black. Available now at the following retailers: Fowl Yoyos, Indignant Return Tops, and others.

Option #3

- The Duckhat Yoyos "Hat-Hat"
- Features: High-quality ball bearing, fingerspin-ready cup
- Colors: Sky-blue, rose-red, puppy-hater black
- Available at Fowl Yoyos, Indignant Return Tops, and others

The first option is terrible for a product description. It's a wall of text that is going to make your customers click on something else. It would make a decent blog post at best. But as for advertising copy, it's just too much.

The second option is a good synopsis and would make a decent product description or a social media post.

The third option is quick, simple and is generally what you want for a product description. A customer can take a quick look at the details and make a decision.

A good approach is to blend the three as needed. If you have a hard time keeping things short and to the point, start a Twitter account. Post a couple of times a day about anything you want. The 280-character limit forces efficiency. I also recommend a program called Hemingway Editor. It's a free web-based program for editing grammar. Write your content, paste it there, and use its live editing features to create direct and to-the-point writing.

If you do want to learn the skill of concise writing, hit the library or YouTube for some writing guides. Pick a product that isn't yours, write up a few different bits of advertising, and then ask your social media community to give you feedback. People on the Internet love to critique writing!

If you are not super confident about your writing, consider hiring out. I have one friend who runs a yoyo brand and swaps a yoyo for advertising copy on each release. He has many skills, but writing isn't one of them.

IMAGES

About 6 months after releasing the production run of The Duck, I looked back and realized that one of colorways had sold substantially better than the other. In hindsight, most of that was down to the photography. The bright, rainbow colors I'd chosen were in shadow, so customers didn't see a fantastically colored yoyo, they saw dull, boring shades. Pictures are a remarkably flexible advertising tool. You can communicate a lot without words. Photography is also an incredibly challenging art form to master. The modern smartphone has provided everyone with an objectively amazing camera in their pocket. What the smartphone doesn't do is tell you how to take a great photo. Here are some tips to get you started.

You need the following:

- **A decent camera** — A reasonably new cell phone or an intro level digital single-lens reflex camera (DSLR) will do.

- **A light box** — An inexpensive one from eBay is fine. You just need a solid background with walls for the light to bounce off of. This reduces shadow and gives you a cleaner picture.

- **Photography lights** — You get what you pay for, but something is better than nothing - even if it's just a pair of angled desk lamps. Having at least two gives you decent control over your photos. The more light you have, the easier it is to take a good photo. Good lighting can compensate for a bad camera, and bad lighting can make your expensive camera take terrible photos.

- **Editing software** — A lot depends on how much you want to learn, but get something basic at least. If using Photoshop sounds too intimidating, load up Paint 3D on your PC (or the Apple equivalent) or grab a free app on your cell phone.

- **Basic knowledge of lighting and photography** — A basic rule of thumb is that strong diffused light is better than direct light. Beginner tip: Avoid having your light source pointing at the camera. The light source should be behind or beside the camera.

Take time to learn some basic editing skills. You need to be able to resize, crop, and adjust brightness/warmth, *etc.* I use a free app on my phone for social media. I'm quickly learning that if I want my business to grow, I need to learn how to create professional quality photos and have started learning basic photoshop skills.

If you choose to learn photography and editing skills yourself, consider a few things. When using images for marketing, consider the purpose. How is the image framed? What is the purpose of your photo? Is it something to throw on Instagram and Facebook as a social media activity filler? Then toss your yoyo on the table beside your coffee cup and snap a pic with your cell phone camera. Take a moment to trim it down, then pop it on Instagram, with a built-in filter. What do you have in mind? A direct advertisement with a call to action? Then you want to aim for better quality. Choose a setting and tone that fits your brand image. Pay attention to lighting and use a higher-quality camera on a tripod. Finish up with some edits to enhance the image and add a few words to drive action.

Stock photos or royalty-free photos can be a useful tool if you need backgrounds or images to go with written posts. Just keep licensing in mind. When you are an individual using images found on Google, odds are the owner won't bother you. But if you pull up a drawing or a photo on a Google image search and use it in your advertising, you are on risky legal ground.

VIDEO

Video quality and use requirements vary between platforms. On Instagram, you are fine with your cell phone camera. For YouTube, you may want something more powerful or versatile. The same key concepts that worked for photography will work for video as well. Again, your keyword is *lighting*. Video is a key component of your marketing. A well-filmed and edited trick compilation video will get shared and watched. Retailers like to have it as an added promo.

- **Lighting** — This is the most important thing to understand. Being outdoors on an overcast day is the easiest way to get good lighting. If you are in a room with one light in the ceiling, at the very least, buy a couple of desk lamps you can set up to point towards you. When I started out, I used a pair of standing lights and leaned them against chairs to light up the corner of my room. This was not a great solution but worked much better than a single ceiling light. A price of US$50 or $60 on Amazon will get you a decent starting setup.

- **Camera** — A cell phone camera can work if you have good lighting. You can get an affordable second-hand GoPro camera off eBay or one of the many GoPro alternatives for as low as US$40 or $50. Still, if you want to produce quality videos, you'll need to shop around for a quality camera.

- **Backdrop** — When it comes to yoyo trick videos, remember that the yoyo and string are the focus. Contrast the background with the yoyo string: black string/white backdrop, white string/black backdrop. Black is pretty standard as long as you have good lighting. When filming a tutorial, you want a solid colored background, with your subject in plain, solid color clothes. The less you have distracting from the yoyo and the string the better the video is. For a trick compilation video, you can have cool scenery as a backdrop. But keep in mind that the busier the background the harder it is to see the string and the yoyo.

- **Editing** — YouTube and Instagram have simple editing options built in, so you can get away with not having a third-party software if you need to. Windows 10 has a built-in editor. Just right-click your file, select "open with," and then select "photos." Click the "edit and create" button and choose "create video with text" to get access to some cut-and-trim features.

If you have an Apple device, you have access to iMovie, which is a powerful tool for the price. I use it on my iPad to put in my logo and make sections slow motion for tutorials.

You don't have to spend a fortune to get some decent software. I asked around, and the #1 recommendation was either Adobe Premiere Elements or Adobe Premiere Rush. At time of writing, Premiere Elements was US$99.99, with Premiere Rush available for US$9.99 per month.

Finally, there is a plethora of apps to choose from. Most are good for simple video editing and are inexpensive. These vary depending on a platform and device, so I recommend reading some reviews or testing the free version before you buy.

Don't let hardware/software "challenges" put you off of using video. A few years ago, I stopped making tutorials because I didn't have time for editing. A friend pointed out that his channel on YouTube consisted almost entirely of videos filmed with his cell phone camera. I tried his method with my tutorials and people loved it. They were bite sized and could be learned in a session. Here is a list of ideas:

- **Trickcircle** — A quick video of your newest trick
- **Tutorial** — Use three cameras and go crazy with multiple angles, or just use your cell phone capturing a single angle and explaining the trick. Make sure you actually teach the trick! A full-speed trick in slow motion is not a tutorial. Remember, there are many more beginners watching tutorials than there are pros, so you don't need long, complex combos to reach customers by teaching.
- **Vlog** — Talk about yoyos, about your life, about your journey making them. Just you talking to the camera works, or have a conversation with a friend/family member/pet. People really love getting to know the people behind their yoyos.
- **Edited trick video** — This is where good equipment is more important. If you don't have the interest or skill set, hire someone else to do so. If money is tight and you can't afford to hire a professional, see whether you can find a local hobby videographer who would be willing to film you doing some tricks. You can cut together a video by yourself or pay for the editing as well. You may even manage some sort of trade. (Yoyos? Yoyo lesson for their kid?)

To conclude, I'd like to remind that you don't need to do everything at once. Start with your comfort zone, then branch out. If you already produce video content on a regular basis, start there and take time to learn writing and photo editing. If you love writing, start with a blog and written reviews. Your content sells your brand, so keep it reasonably high quality and consistent. That way, when the time comes to send it out to customers, they'll be excited to see it.

CHAPTER 5 - MAILING LIST

Your mailing list is one of the best tools you have for marketing. If you are careful as you collect email addresses, people join your list because they are interested in what you do. Collecting and curating such a list is work, but it will pay off. The benefit is that you have direct contact with people who want to buy what you sell. This is a lot better than gambling on social media posts, looking for customers.

The worst way to manage a mailing list is through a spreadsheet and your personal email address. It's time consuming, looks unprofessional, and you will spend too much time tracking unsubscribes. You will also run afoul of spam filters. Your email service provider may also limit the number of outgoing emails you can send at a time or in a day.

The solution is to use an email marketing service. I'm not going to provide a comparison chart here, as the available options and their features change constantly. Mailchimp is the one I use; I've also heard good things about MailerLite and ConvertKit. Wix, Squarespace, Shopify, and Weebly offer built-in mailing list and marketing management. They also offer third-party integrations (options the build themselves into your website), as does Shopify and WordPress. I'll discuss Mailchimp's features with the understanding that these features are similar to what you will find on other platforms.

UNDERSTAND THE RULES

There are many ways to collect addresses for your mailing list. It's important that when you do so, you follow the rules and laws that are in place.

Read the rules of your mailing service provider. Get to know laws around spam and data collection in both your country and the countries where you will do business. For example, in 2018, the European Union launched the General Data Protection Regulation (GDPR). This puts a limit on how much businesses may use customer information without direct and clear consent. I'm in Canada, but I have mailing list subscribers in Europe, so I need to know how to follow these rules. Other countries have their own variants of this law as well.

This step doesn't need to be overwhelming. If you treat subscriber information the way you would like your email address to be treated, you will likely be fine. Collect email addresses for marketing purposes directly from the owners of the email accounts and make it very clear what you will be using them for.

The good news is that services like Mailchimp offer forms and information to help. Create a signup form to add to your website, or a link from your social media. State what you intend to do with the information directly on the signup form. Then, you can be assured that people signing up know what they are in for and have given consent to receive your marketing emails. If you do have that Excel spreadsheet you've been collecting addresses on, you can use Mailchimp to send them an opt-in email. The best practice is to use a double opt-in system, where people sign up and then get an email asking them to confirm their subscription. This ensures that the owner of the account has actually signed up, and it double-checks that they actually want to be on your list.

Email providers like Gmail and Outlook have sophisticated anti-spam software. If many people report spam coming from your email address, your future emails end up in people's spam folders where they aren't opened. Systems like Mailchimp also track your unsubscribes and spam report rate and can block or ban your account.

The best way to prevent subscribes and spam reports is to collect a list properly and regularly send quality content.

COLLECTING ADDRESSES

Your customers are the first place to look for subscribers. You can't add customers without permission, but you can send them an invitation to subscribe. You can also add a step to your checkout process where they choose to sign up. Your website can feature a signup form, either embedded somewhere or as a pop-up.

You can also run a contest. Create a landing page (either with Mailchimp or directly on your website). Create a content post on social media and tell people they just need to sign up to enter. Keep in mind that many people sign up only for the shot at a prize and that many will unsubscribe later. This is still worth doing, as some will stick around and eventually make a purchase.

Finally, you can offer a free gift. Giving away a sticker pack or something similar works but still costs you money and time. Digital content is easier. If you create tutorials or guides, do a miniseries that's available to subscribers only. You can upload videos to YouTube and set them so that they are viewable with a link only. You can also create a password-protected section of your website that's just for subscriber news.

WHAT TO GIVE AWAY?

How much time do you spend reading a marketing email that hits your inbox? I know. I usually give it a quick look and then move on unless something grabs my attention. I try to craft my email newsletters and announcements with this in mind. I use headings and sections to make key information easy to spot, with details available if people want to read on. Include images, but keep them formatted small so they don't take time to load or use up mobile data.

When I choose to sign up for a mailing list, I do so because I want to receive information. Don't be afraid to contact the people on your mailing list. That's literally what they've signed up for. Do keep in mind what makes *you* unsubscribe from a list. I know that I will leave a list if it's a deluge of repetitive sales emails.

Here are a few strategies to keep your subscribers engaged:

1. Your content

Send a newsletter featuring trick videos or blog posts. If you don't already create content, consider doing so. Simple videos sharing knowledge or those of you doing tricks are great. High quality is better, but don't let that stop you. You are bound to have some knowledge to share. Your team of sponsored players can also create content for you. (See the next section on sponsorship.)

2. Share other people's content

Choose a notepad app for your phone and make a note any time you spot a tutorial, a bit of wisdom, or an article on a yoyo news site. Work those into your newsletters. Don't just talk about your yoyos. Mention strings and accessories you like, or cool yoyo art or clothing you've picked up. If you are willing to talk about other brands, you become more trustworthy when you talk about yours. Remember the human face of the brand.

3. Giveaways

I like to periodically run a giveaway that is exclusive to my mailing list. This serves as both a *thank-you* to my subscribers and a way to re-engage people who don't open your newsletters often. You can use Mailchimp's built-in features to track the contact info of the people that have clicked and then draw names from that. Your next newsletter can include the name of the winner. Just double-check that they don't mind you sharing their name. If they do, you can still announce, "The prize was awarded, but the winner asked to remain anonymous."

4. Discounts

An occasional mailing list discount or a two-for-one deal can be a powerful tool if you need a bump in your sales to finance the next run. Just use this tool very sparingly. If you offer a discount every month, customers will just be waiting for the deal instead of shopping when they are ready. You want customers trained to pay a full price. I give new subscribers a one-time "buy two get one free" discount code built into my onboarding series (more on this to follow). That email outlines my "12 months, 12 yoyos" promotion and is a way for new subscribers to get caught up on their Rain City Skills collection. I try to avoid percentage discounts on yoyos and instead go with "get a free bearing" or "get 50% off a t-shirt if you buy a yoyo."

The key to remember with your content is that you want a regular schedule of content that is quick and easy to digest and doesn't overload your subscribers. If a monthly newsletter works for you, stick with that. If you have enough content to share that you can do up a weekly newsletter, that's great too. A good tip is to pick a day that is a newsletter day and create your email in advance. And don't forget to edit, edit, edit!

ADVANCED FEATURES

Automations

Once you've set up your mailing list, you want to craft an automated welcome email which will be sent as soon as someone signs up. If you've offered a free gift for signing up, this is where you can give it. An automatic welcome email is a great interactive step. Keep the content general so you don't have to change it. Don't try to make a sale right away, instead welcome your subscriber(s) and promise to be in touch soon.

With an upgraded paid plan, you can also set up what's called an "onboarding sequence." This is a series of emails that go out automatically at intervals after that first welcome email. This gives new subscribers a chance to get to know you. Part of my onboarding sequence is a free PDF that tells the Rain City Skills origin story.

Keep in mind that you don't want to overload customers. If you spread your sequence out over a month or two, they remind people they signed up.

Analytics

One of the many benefits of having a service like Mailchimp managing your mailing list is information. Are people reading your emails? Clicking on links? If the email is an inbox and doesn't get opened, Mailchimp tracks that. If you have put a link to your store or to a product, Mailchimp tracks whether the link was clicked. If you've put out a product release email and no one clicked on the link, it might be the time to re-think your format.

You can also re-send your email to those on your list who didn't open it. Don't do this more than once per email though. You don't want to risk being reported as spam. Keep in mind that your *open* rate will be low. If you get 20 per cent to 30 per cent on an email, you are doing well. Don't get too worried about that. The emails still keep crossing their inbox, reminding them you are out there.

I cannot overstate how important a mailing list is. Without it, each customer is a new customer every time. With it, every customer becomes a potential repeat customer. Keep them engaged with consistent, high-quality content, but don't overwhelm them. Start inviting people to join your list early and often. You'll be glad you did.

CHAPTER 6 - SOCIAL MEDIA MARKETING

Keywords

Feed — A stream of content that social media sites present to you, based on your preferences and previous behavior on the site

Post — Sharing content (kind of like Post-it Notes stuck on a public bulletin board)

Hashtags or tags — The "#" symbol placed before various words to help sort content on Facebook, Twitter, Instagram, and other sites (If someone on Instagram searches for #yoyo, they get a list of all recent posts including that hashtag. But they won't include every mention of the word *yoyo*.)

Algorithm — A computer term for the program that sorts and organizes information on a site (These usually tailor your experience on a site, based on your past actions.)

Like — Social media currency (Viewers can "like" your post to indicate approval.)

Follower/subscriber — A person who chooses to have your posts appear in their feed.

Filter — A preset photo edit

Direct/Private/Personal Message (DM/PM) — A message seen only by you and the sender/receiver

Organic reach — The degree to which your content is seen without your having to spend any money

The Internet is an overwhelming place. More people than you could ever interact with create more content than any human could view in a lifetime. The good news is that you are already out there. The key to remember for a boutique brand is that you need to be a person first, a business professional second, and a salesman a very distant third. I'm not going to re-invent the wheel here. Most platforms make it easy to get started. But if you get stuck, hop onto YouTube and search "how to set up a __________ account" for any social media platforms you want to try out.

What follows here is an outline of getting set up. Don't get overwhelmed by this list. Odds are you are already using at least one of these; start there. Add more as you have the time and energy. An active presence in one place is far more valuable than spotty interactions in many. Here are 3 tips that will help you across platforms.

1. Scheduled content

YouTube and Facebook both have built-in scheduling features. You can set a YouTube video to "private" with a scheduled time to change it to "public." Your posts from your Facebook business page also offer the option. There's a little drop-down menu right above the "share now" button with a clock. Both of these allow you to upload a week's worth of content in one sitting and then forget about it.

I use the free version of a third-party scheduler called Hootsuite. I've also used one called Buffer. You create content, schedule the post through Hootsuite or Buffer for all of your social media, and then select a date/time to release it. Then you can forget about it and work on other parts of your business. Daily content for the sake of visibility posts are out of the way, leaving you to focus on running your business. I use a scheduler for my generic visibility posts and then try to throw in a few specific day-to-day things.

I try once a week to dedicate twenty minutes to taking a bunch of yoyo pictures and to giving them basic sizing and editing. Then I add a bit of text and schedule two weeks' worth. These are the equivalent of a billboard ad. They are there; they cross the feed and disappear. It's a fair bit of work for a thing that disappears, but they add up to consistent visibility.

2. Know your demographics

I poked around some 2018 statistics on a variety of websites and noticed the following broad generalizations: Facebook and YouTube lean a little more toward older yoyoers; Instagram and Snapchat toward those younger. Facebook and YouTube sit around the 50:50 mobile-to-desktop use; Snapchat and Instagram are mobile dominant.

What does this mean for you? If you are focused on high-end expensive collectables, you want to know where the older yoyoers with money are. If you make a competition-driven yoyo, you want to target younger yoyoers. Beginner yoyo? Kids and their parents.

The fact that mobile devices are used over half the time for most social media use tells you to craft your content for short snippets of attention. The three minutes waiting in an elevator, ten minutes between classes, ten minutes hiding in the bathroom, a few moments avoiding work, *etc.*

I've read that there are ideal times to post content, depending on your industry. I doubt that anyone has done yoyoer-specific research, but it's worth considering what time your customers are likely online. If your customers are high school students, 9 a.m. isn't your best bet. Likewise, if you target the casual older yoyoer, 11:00 p.m. is probably too late. Also keep in mind time zones. If your customers are in California, and you post content at 9 a.m. EST, it is 6 a.m. for them and they are probably still asleep. This ties back to scheduling. I generally have time to make social media posts while on the bus to and from work, but I schedule them to release during peak hours.

3. Analytics

Your best friend in marketing is information. How do you know the best way to spend your time? By paying attention to the information each platform can provide. Facebook, Instagram, YouTube — they each offer you the ability to see when your customers are online, what they interact with, and how your efforts pay off week to week. This also gives you a basis from which to experiment. Did you have a successful post? Look at what time you posted it and compare to similar content at different times. I find that I get the most attention on Instagram mid-week during the day, but that's also when I'm most likely to be throwing random content online. This tells me I should look at expanding my posting times and scheduling content for non-peak times to figure out whether there are better times for me to post.

I've broken down this section, based on each social media platform I use and the strategies I've had success with. Keep in mind that the social media world is bigger than this and is ever evolving. These suggestions and tips will need fine tuning for your niche.

FACEBOOK

If you aren't already on Facebook, you may need to be. It isn't the only place to find yoyoers, but a lot of us are there. The setup is pretty easy. If you don't want your personal life to appear on Facebook, do what I did and create an account just for yoyos.

If you are already on Facebook and want your personal profile to stay personal, spend some time working on your settings. Find your settings and look at "timeline and tagging." If you want your personal profile to be private, limit these options. Under privacy, you can change your settings from "Everyone sees everything" to "Only me." If you are like me and are on Facebook for the yoyo business only, keep these open.

Once you are on Facebook, you need to know about **five places** you'll be working with: your feed, your timeline, pages, groups, and your story.

1. Feed

It is the first thing you see when you log in. It's a list of posts and discussions that the Facebook algorithm has decided you want to see. You can teach the algorithm what you want it to show you by following pages, hiding uninteresting posts, and clicking or commenting on content you like. Be careful not to waste your day endlessly scrolling. If you use Facebook for business and nothing else, ignore the memes, politics, and drama. Just interact with yoyo-related content. Your customers will see content in their feed if they have followed your page and regularly interacted with your content.

2. Timeline

When you make a "new post" at the top of your feed, it is stored on your timeline. Assuming you opted to keep your timeline settings public, you can make your posts be seen by people on your friends list and anyone who checks your profile. Kind of. Again, this depends on who interacts with you, so your reach is very limited. Keep in mind that anything you "share" ends up here, and when potential customers want to check out who this person selling yoyos is, they will go look through your profile. Controversial content may put off potential customers. I've lost a couple of sales because I made the mistake of getting into a heated political discussion that accomplished nothing but the alienation of a customer. I suggest that you avoid such discussions. They create nothing but frustration and eat up a lot of time that could be used for furthering your business.

3. Pages

You will need a business page. At time of writing, a page is useful as a platform for managing your paid advertisements, but little else. A tiny percentage of what you post will find its way organically into customers' feeds. But that's a percentage who still see your content. This doesn't mean you shouldn't put effort here. Quite the opposite. You need your customers to engage with your page so you can target them with ads. So, posting regular content and sharing it to groups is important.

4. Groups

Groups are created by individuals and managed for a variety of purposes. Interested in fly fishing? Find a fly-fishing group. Sunbeam toasters from the 1950s? There's a group for that. Groups are the best way to be sure like-minded people see your brand. Be very careful to be aware of each group's rules around the content. A quick way to get banned from a group with hundreds of potential customers is to jump in with "Hey buy my product!" posts, especially if the rules state "no advertising".

You can also create a group if you see an opening. I created the group "Offstring Yoyo Nuts" because there wasn't a group for offstring yoyoers. I recommend finding the "Yoyo BST & Talk" group to get you started. From there, you can branch out based on interest. Just make sure to read the group rules first. They are usually in the "About" section found on the left sidebar on your desktop. You can also find it by clicking the group title on your mobile device.

5. Story

Stories appear at the top of your feed. They are transient content, images, and video that stay up for a day. These are worth paying attention to if for no other reason than their sitting in that prime piece of real estate. A story exists for twenty-four hours and then disappears. This makes it ideal for more casual content. A quick video reflecting on something yoyo related that day, a quick clip of a Canada goose chasing you with murder on its mind, or just a few nice photos of your latest release. It's also a great spot for release announcements: "24 hours until the Duckhat "Fishbowl" releases!" More than anything, these posts are going to be exactly what the name says, a piece of your brand's story.

OK, now that the tour is over, here are some tips for getting your message out.

Paid Ads

I'll speak more to this in a later chapter, but for now, I'll recommend caution. It's easy to throw away money on paid ads and somewhat difficult to make them pay off. When you start out, most of your advertising is going to be hands-on community involvement.

Photo, Video, or Text?

Yes. To all of it. Keep in mind the tips I've mentioned previously and keep in mind the short attention span of people on Facebook. When you make a post, the first three to four lines will be visible. After that, people will have to click to read. Make those first few lines appear as an engaging hook and put your useful and engaging content after that. Tell bits of your story, review things, ask questions, answer questions. Above all, pay attention to your grammar and spelling!

Use photos to get attention and draw people to read your content or click on a link. Good images get shared. Images with a clear call to action get attention. Post up two prototypes, and poll to decide which to produce. Do the same with colorways options, bearings, *etc.* Pictures catch the eye and drive interaction. You can even craft and share the occasional meme, joke, or bit of silliness. Just be sure whatever you do fits the image you want your brand to present.

Create videos that are short and easy to watch. You can use links to your YouTube or Instagram, but content posted directly into Facebook will get more organic reach than a link will. I've read in a few places that Facebook is the #2 place people view videos after YouTube. A thirty-to-sixty-second trick video seems to be just right. But if you have something innovative to offer, go to town!

Go live. It's an option when you start a post. Yoyo and answer questions on camera, live stream the million hours you spend testing and packaging your yoyos. If you do your own design work, live stream the creative process. You won't get a whole lot of response right away, but a half-dozen people watching your boxing up the yoyos are going to be the first in line on the release day. I once live streamed myself packing up yoyo orders. One viewer made the decision to buy a yoyo then and there and was delighted to see me pack up his order on-screen! Any way you can write people into your story is worth putting some time into.

INSTAGRAM

Instagram lends itself beautifully to yoyoing. Photos and videos are the centerpiece of the platform, being perfect for yoyo photos and trick videos. It took me a while to get the hang of it, but I've found a lot of yoyoers who aren't on Facebook, especially younger players.

It's a low-text zone. You have to say most of what you want to say with an image. You get about two sentences in your description. So, treat it like Twitter and keep it short. Text is best used as a call to action.

Instagram feeds you posts, based on whom you follow, how often you interact with their content, and how recently they have posted. If you follow a lot of people, make sure to check in with the ones you want to see on a regular basis and throw them a like. Keep in mind that this goes both ways. If you want people to see your posts, your content needs to encourage interaction.

If you decide to post a picture of your yoyo beside a cup of coffee, don't just talk about the yoyo. Ask people to comment on their favorite hot beverage or coffee shop.

Like Facebook, you need people to take action on your posts if you want your content to be featured in their feed. You can also use the "stickers" option in the "Stories" section to add interactive text to your images.

You have three main places to upload content: your gallery, stories, and IGTV. Each one serves a different function, and you should be hitting them all if you can.

1. Gallery

Your gallery is a place where new fans can get a snapshot of your brand. I've seen some galleries that alternate images with plain text posts. They look really clean, and it's a great way to create a professional image that matches up with your brand colors. My gallery is a mess of whatever I've had time to throw on there. You can post images and videos (up to one minute) here. Keep in mind that your images need to be square. Either take them with your phone in portrait or crop them.

The gallery is also the place where you can share some contact information and a brief bio and can upload a profile photo. This is also the only place you can put a web link. Keep the link up to date. It can be used in a couple ways: (1) At the very least, put a link to your website; (2) A more advanced use is to post a picture of content or a call to action in your gallery with the comment "link in bio". Example: Post a picture of your latest release with a bit of text stating: "available now from the Duckhat Yoyos store, link in bio." This is useful if you keep it up to date. But if you are prone to forgetfulness, I suggest just keeping a link to your store instead.

Instagram is easy to navigate. Click the plus sign in the bottom middle of the home screen to post content. You will see three options: gallery, photo, and video. Gallery allows you to upload photos or videos from your device. I use this option, so I can edit photos before uploading. You can also upload multiple photos at once. When you announce a new yoyo, you can post pics of each colorway in the same post. Start with a group shot, then do a zoomed-in photo of each.

The photo option allows you to take a photo with the built-in camera software. The video button does the same, but it's different from your regular camera. You have to hold the button to record. This makes it less useful for filming yourself doing tricks. It does have a fun feature though. You can press and hold to film something for a few seconds, let go, then start again. Repeat multiple times until you have collected up to a minute. This is handy if you are at a contest. You can take little video clips of a bunch of people doing tricks and upload them as a single video.

Instagram offers a few built-in editing options. With a photo, you can adjust the basic settings (brightness, contrast, saturation), which are generally a necessity with your average poorly lit photos. You can also add a preset filter. These are fun to play with and get you different effects. Video has filters and gives you the option to choose the cover image (useful if your trick video starts with you making an awkward face). What you can't do is edit your logo into the beginning of your video without using a third-party app.

2. Stories

Stories are more ephemeral content. After you post your story, it stays active for twenty-four hours and then disappears. You can save up to four story posts. There are a ton of options to play around with here, so tap the button and test it out! The "stickers" option built into stories is a surprisingly versatile marketing tool. Here are several good ones to experiment with:

- **<u>Poll</u>**:
  Post two colorways of your yoyo and ask viewers to vote on their favorite.
  What do you prefer: 1a or 5a?
  Did Jeremy McKay deliver the best-ever yoyo contest performance at the 2019 Canadian National Yoyo Contest? "Yes" or "He's crazy"

- **<u>Question</u>**:
  How are you feeling today?
  What song are you listening to?
  What yoyo are you carrying?
  What is your favorite song to yoyo to?

- **<u>Countdown</u>**: It's almost release day! Let's get people thinking about it. It also helps with managing time zones to have a countdown timer going.

The key with stories is to pop in and post something on-brand and engaging every day.

3. IGTV

Finally, you have IGTV. To use this feature, click the little TV icon beside the direct message icon in the top corner of your screen. This is a newer function where you are able to upload videos of up to ten minutes in length. I've been using this as a platform for my vlog as well as tutorials and longer trick videos. This functions almost as a separate app within Instagram, so it needs its own content. You can share your IGTV content to your stories for cross promotion. My best suggestion here is that if you already use YouTube for longer videos, post them here as well.

Hashtags

Your visibility to others will revolve around two things: (1) interacting with others' content and (2) the use of hashtags. Instead of groups or pages, Instagram revolves around hashtags. Getting to know what hashtags are being used in the yoyo community will help you find potential customers. I'm not going to list a bunch here because they change constantly. Start with the search function and look for "#yoyos" and "#yoyotricks." Pick some posts getting a lot of views and look at the hashtags used in them. Pay attention to content though. "#yoyo" is full of non-yoyo content. Open a notepad and keep a list.

You can use up to thirty hashtags in a post. I don't have an answer on how many to use. I've read articles that say "keep it to five or less," and I've seen articles arguing "use all thirty." Before you start posting pictures of yoyos with a wall of tags in the text box, consider a few things.

Hashtag Tips:
- **Don't** mix your hashtags into your text (Check out my #yoyo from #raincityskills). Put them after your text. (Check out my yoyo from Rain City Skills. #yoyo #raincityskills)

- **Don't** use #yoyotrick when posting a picture of a yoyo or #raincityskills when posting a picture of a "Duckhat" yoyo. Make sure the tags describe what is in the picture.

- **Do** use #beach if your yoyo is on the beach or #justinbieber if your photo was taken at the Justin Bieber concert. This expands your reach, and you never know when you might find a Bieber fan who gets crazy into yoyos!

Instagram's algorithm tracks accounts that use the same hashtags in every post and reduces the post's visibility. So, mix it up. Get yourself a list of thirty to forty yoyo-related tags and mix'n'match them, based on content. Blend-in non-yoyo tags that describe other things in the picture. This gives you the benefit of being seen by non-yoyoers, and you never know when one of them will get curious. Being someone's first experience with yoyos has value.

As I sit writing this, I'm posting a picture of my yoyo beside my cup of coffee at the coffee shop. I'll use the following tags:

#yoyo, #todaysthrow, #yotography, #delayneyscoffee, #bookstagram, #writersofinstagram #coffee #fedora, #englishbay, #nonfictionwriting, #raincityskills, #mryoyothrower, #workbreak, #EDC, #pocketdump, #workbreak.

Repost

Instagram doesn't allow you to "share" other people's posts, but there are a few tools to get around this limitation. I use an Android app called "repost," which copies an Instagram post and then puts it up on your profile. Part of the process copies the text of the original post to your clipboard, so you can add it to your post and give credit. The best practice is to always check with the owner of the content before you repost it. You don't want to be stealing content. I use this tool to repost my sponsored player's content to my brand's Instagram or to share images posted by fans.

YOUTUBE

As a Grade 2 teacher, I can tell you that YouTube is slowly putting me out of work. OK, that's a bit of an exaggeration, but not by much. It is where millions of people go to get their questions answered and to learn new skills, one of which is definitely yoyoing. I once lead my class through a project of creating books and selling them to raise money for charity. At least a third of my class spent their time on YouTube, learning how to draw characters for the coloring books.

You can use YouTube with nothing more than your smartphone camera and YouTube's built-in editing features. Or you can load up on an expensive camera and editing gear. When you film, keep in mind that any commercial music you use is likely under copyright and can limit your visibility. YouTube has a range of built-in royalty-free music you can use. Or if you have the skills, you can even record your own!

Once you've uploaded the video, you need to add a title, description, and tags. Make the title catchy but clear about the content ("yoyo trick tutorial – name" or "discussion: why yoyos are better than ducks"). Your description starts with a very brief description. You can also use this space for promotion (Yoyo used – the "Duckhat"; yoyo brand – "Wingclip"). A major benefit of YouTube over Instagram is that you can add clickable links in the description, but you need the full URL with the "http://" (for example, http://www.raincityskills.com, NOT www.raincityskills.com).

Tags help YouTube point people to your video. One way to figure out what will work is to start a search in the YouTube search bar. Type "yoyo," hit the space bar, see what comes up as options. These are good things to tag, since they are the things people actually search for. Don't forget to tag your personal brand and specifics of what is in the video. When you post tricks or tutorials, keep in mind potential new yoyos when you name your trick. One of my most popular yoyo trick videos is called Murphy's Law. A lot of the views are probably accidental, but you never know when one of those will turn into a fan!

Playlists are a great tool as well. If you don't want to maintain a website page indexing your videos, create playlists. If you have sponsored players, create a playlist for each of them. Tutorials, trickcircle videos, and vlogs will keep people watching your channel and remembering your brand come shopping time.

Finally, scheduling. Some of the third-party scheduler apps will post to YouTube for you, but I prefer the built-in scheduler. When you upload your video, you have the option of setting it to "public," "private," or "unlisted."

"Public" means everyone can see it, which is what you want most of the time. "Unlisted" gives you the option of uploading a video that is seen by only those people who have the link. I use that when I want to give my mailing list a sneak peek at something coming up. "Private" means no one sees it but you. But it gives you the option of scheduling when it becomes public.

REDDIT

Reddit is a different animal. It is organized by subreddit. A subreddit is like a Facebook group. The subreddit for yoyos is r/throwers (you can search that directly on Google). This is a trickier platform to be a business on. Direct sale and promotional posts are discouraged except in the pinned "Weekly Buy, Sell and Trade" thread. I get away with the promotional posts because I have spent years building a reputation for contributing to the community. It's a fine line though. I did get into trouble a few years ago when I started blogging. I got accused of writing advertising copy and over posting it.

You can interact with others in four main ways: (1) make a post, (2) comment on a post, (3) up/downvote a post, or (4) send a direct message.

Share the same kind of content as any other social media site when you create a post. You have the option of text, image/video, or a link. The link option allows readers to click the title of the post and go straight to the outside page. This function works for images, YouTube videos, and anything else that's coming in from an outside source. If you want engagement on reddit, put a question in the title and encourage discussion.

When you upload a photo, it shows up right in the feed, so a good photo is an attention grabber. Video works the same. As with Facebook, you are better off uploading directly than linking a YouTube video.

Commenting on other posts is a good way to gain goodwill and get your name known, especially if your comments are helpful and encouraging. If someone has trouble with a trick, share a tutorial (either yours or someone else's). If they have questions and you have answers, speak up!

Find the little "mail" icon in the top right corner of your computer screen or bottom right on the app screen. This is where you find private messages. These are great if you want to connect with an individual privately.

Visibility on reddit is a lot more democratic than on other sites. Instead of an algorithm deciding what you see, other users vote on what they think is valuable to the community. To the left of your post there is a pair of arrows (one up, one down) and a number between them. If you post something uninteresting, it'll get either no votes or "downvotes." Downvoting pushes a post down the feed quickly. If your post gets a lot of "upvotes," it'll stay higher up in the feed and get more views. When I post a tutorial, I usually get at least a day before it disappears to the second page. Take time to upvote the things you like so that they stay visible for others.

My most successful post on reddit was an older promo video that hadn't received much attention at the time. When preparing this section, I uploaded it to reddit to test the functional difference between a direct upload and a video link. I titled it "Ignore this, testing something." As it turned out, that was a great title, as nothing sparks human curiosity better than being told not to be curious! I ended up leaving the post up because people were enjoying it so much. The fact that it was a well-edited funny video with some great tricks definitely helped.

All in all, reddit is a good place to have a presence. There are many yoyoers who don't use Facebook or Instagram. Just move-in slowly and get known before you start trying to make sales.

FORUMS

Yoyoexpert.com is one of the biggest marketplaces for yoyos in the world. It also hosts a yoyo-dedicated forum. Before Facebook, forums were the place where most yoyoers hung out on the Internet. Some forums are still on the web, but Yoyoexpert is definitely one to pay attention to. The biggest benefit of being part of a yoyo-specific environment is getting the opportunity of having a younger yoyoer account.

The forum is divided into categories ranging from general discussion topics to tricks to manufacturer news. Take some time to get a feel for it and decide whether you want to spend time building a name in this community. Based on the publicly displayed numbers, this is a busy forum that could be worth your time. If you plan to sell yoyos through Yoyoexpert's retail store, a presence here is a must.

The biggest challenge to social media marketing is managing your time. It's really easy to get sucked into the Facebook feed and end up scrolling for an hour when you should be working. Scheduling your content is a good way to avoid that. Scheduling your time is an even better way. My best advice is to log out of your apps on your phone. Pick three to four times per day when you plan to sit down for a pre-determined period and comment, reply, like, share, and engage with customers. Then log out again and get back to other things. If logging out isn't possible, limit your notifications. A year ago, I realized that my day was constantly interrupted unnecessarily. I didn't need to know when people replied on Facebook or liked an Instagram post, or when I got yet another marketing email from a random retailer. So I turned off most of the notifications, leaving a few - like direct messages - active. I now try to designate times to check in. I don't always succeed, but I'm much better than I used to be. Every time I mindlessly pull my phone out of my pocket, I ask myself, "What are you doing right now to improve yourself or further your business?" Then, more often than not, I close Facebook and open a book.

The biggest key to being successful on social media is consistency. Start where you are at and create a consistent schedule to release content. Even if it's just a picture and a few words every day. Don't kill yourself trying to use every platform listed above and the dozens of others that are out there. Start small and consistent, build a following, then expand from there.

CHAPTER 7 - ONLINE GIVEAWAY

The giveaway is a standard marketing practice in the yoyo world (and in most industries). This section covers some ways to run contests on different platforms to generate attention for a new release, collect information, or build goodwill.

Start with some questions.

Why are you giving a yoyo away? Are you collecting email addresses, likes for your Facebook pages, subscriptions for your YouTube, or followers on

Instagram? Are you trying to highlight a new release? There are ways to do all these at once, but sometimes you want to target a particular market. Most importantly, keep track of what you accomplish each time, so you can measure success against cost. A yoyo is a high value item and you might find the same results with an accessory or other gift.

What are you giving away, and what value does it hold? This is important for two reasons:

- understanding *your* cost when setting your goal and deciding whether the campaign was successful (If your goal is page likes, well-targeted Facebook or Instagram ads may be a better decision.)
- perceived value (Your level of engagement will increase with the value of the giveaway, to a point.) I recall giving away two B-grades of a $65 yoyo. They had minor flaws in the finish, so their value was closer to $50 each. One person commented, "That's a lot of work for a b-grade." The total amount of effort required to enter was minimal (maybe five minutes) for a chance at a $50 yoyo. This negative response points to a market full of people who are inundated with contests and aren't willing to work too hard to enter.

Who is your target market? Knowing your market tells you where to apply most of your effort. Facebook is used by all age groups, but people in their 30s–50s are more likely to be on YouTube than on Instagram or Snapchat. The opposite is true for younger people, who are more likely to be on Instagram, Snapchat, or Twitter. Figure out where your target yoyo group spends their time.

How are you going to manage your giveaway to get the most bang for your buck? You need to make sure that whatever you decide is manageable. Instructions to submit a five-minute trick video will be met with crickets unless you are giving away a car. Watching and judging submissions can also eat a lot of your time. Asking for a video with a single trick is a lower bar for entry. People can film that on their phone and upload in a moment. A "Like this post and comment" contest on Facebook is easy for people to enter and is easy to keep track of.

Each platform has different rules. Facebook and Instagram have clear guidelines. Also, instructions like "tag a friend to enter" or "share to your timeline" are actually against the rules. These rules change, so keep up to date. A quick search will bring you to Instagram, Facebook, or YouTube pages outlining contest restrictions and guidelines, which generally prohibit anything that affects analytics (like, comment, subscribe, view video, *etc.*).

Don't forget to consider local laws. You likely aren't allowed to run a contest that requires a purchase to enter, without a special license. You also want to be careful of trademarks and copyright. I don't have all the answers, and policies change, so please make sure you know the rules before you get started.

Finally, remember that a giveaway is part of the 20 percent ask, not the 80 percent share. You give away a free yoyo to one person, but the rest give your time and attention for nothing.

So how should you run a giveaway? Your "why" will direct your decision. Here are a few options I've used with varying levels of success.

SUBMIT A VIDEO

This one can be a lot of work on your part, depending on how you pick a winner. If you choose a random winner, based on a "did you submit a video" criteria, you don't even have to watch them. If you choose to judge them, based on skill, creativity, humor, or difficulty, you'll be watching a lot of videos. You aren't going to get the same number of responses that a simpler contest will get you, but you will garner more relevant responses. I use this type of giveaway only rarely. It's a good way to reward your fan base, since they are the ones most likely to respond.

To do a "submit a video" giveaway, you have a few choices, depending on platform. I suggest you start with a picture of the prize, with the rules written on the picture. Post that everywhere applicable. The easiest thing to do on your end is having them upload a video to their social media of choice and then send you a link. Creating a form in Google docs and sticking a link on your website will take you the least amount of effort. Make it a simple form, asking only for their name and a link. This allows you to include multiple platforms.

Example: Blog Post

Enter the Duckhat Video contest. Upload a 30-second trick video to any platform with the title "Duckhat Yoyo Contest." Use the following hashtags: #duckhatlyfe, #Wingclipyoyo, and #trickcircle

1. Name and email address
2. Link to your video
3. Fill out the form below with a link to your post

Please share the contest link with your friends!

The linked form will consist of their name, their email address, and a consent option for their video or image to be reposted by you. I did this with a coloring contest. One of my sponsored players, Waylon Crase, took up digital art and drew most of an alien as part of our promotional campaign for "The SETI" yoyo. He struggled with the arms and had the idea of running a contest where people finished the drawing for him. People downloaded the image and shared it. I gave them a week and received nine submissions, which was actually better than expected with such a high bar for entry. Most importantly, people had fun and shared their pictures with our hashtags!

If you want to target Instagram exclusively, make use of a hashtag. Use the search feature to come up with a hashtag not in use, like #duckhatyoyocontest. Then make one of the criteria for entry that all videos use that hashtag as well as your brand's tag. This way, you can just search your contest tag and scan through the videos there.

Announce the winner far and wide. If you have sponsored players, have them share the post. You want to maximize the social credit from your perceived altruism. One big benefit of a video contest is that those videos usually stay online. If one of your criteria is to make the title of the video "Duckhat yoyo contest," that's free advertising. If you keep a list of submissions, you can go back later and use them for advertising. Share a link with the comment "Check out Bob's video from our contest last month, what a great trick!" That way, you can maximize the effect you get in exchange for giving away a valuable yoyo. If you plan to do this, it's good to either put a note in the contest rules or get permission from each player.

LIKE AND COMMENT

Facebook

Once upon a time, you could include "Like our page," "Tag a friend," and "Share this post." Those conditions against the rules now. Below are a few suggestions that were allowed at time of writing.

- "Like this post" — the simplest contest. This will get you the most reach but the least quality. Pull up a list of the people who "liked" the post and do a random number draw.
- "Comment on this post" — a slightly higher bar, but not by much. You can add a question (*What's your favorite Duckhat yoyo?*), a fill-in the blank (*My favorite yoyo string is_________*), or a caption contest (*Caption this picture*). The last one can either be a random draw, or you can add a rule like "the funniest caption wins."
- "Post a photo comment" — a higher bar for entry, but you are likely to get people interacting with each other's photos or sharing the post. This can be serious (post a picture of the best yoyo) or fun (post your favorite kid-friendly meme).

Instagram

This type of giveaway is as valid on Instagram, although I again recommend you check the current rules. You can ask people to follow your profile and like/comment on your picture. You are also supposed to include a statement that Instagram is in no way involved in the giveaway. With Instagram you are best off putting at least some of the contest information in your picture. Don't rely on people reading the text below it.

Reddit

For Reddit, you are limited to comments, as you aren't allowed to ask for upvotes. The r/throwers group isn't super friendly to marketing. My suggestion is get in there, contribute and build a strong reputation, then ask politely if you can run a give-away.

YouTube

YouTube has strict rules. You aren't allowed to ask for likes, views, dislikes, subscribes, or comments — essentially anything that would artificially change their metrics. Technically, all you are allowed to do is ask people to view your channel or submit a video to you. That doesn't mean you shouldn't do a giveaway; just consider the best way to use that platform. There's no reason you can't use YouTube to direct people to your website, to comment on a blog post, or to subscribe to your mailing list.

POST A PICTURE

Make sure you follow the rules around tagging things that are in pictures. Instagram and Facebook policies prohibit tagging anything on anyone not actually in the image. On Facebook, the easiest way to work with this one is to have entrants post a picture in the comments of your contest post. On Instagram, you need to have them post a picture and then use your hashtag to identify it. You can specify a title (Duckhat yoyo contest #duckhatyoyo, #3duckcontest).

Example: "The new Duckhat yoyo 'The Melon Mallard' releases Friday. Comment a picture of a strange hat."

ANSWER A SHORT SURVEY

One method of entry is to use Google Forms or a similar program to ask a question or two. Perhaps you are researching names for your next release or deciding on colors? Trying to figure out the average age of your customers? Give away a yoyo or an accessory in exchange. Just keep it really short — one to three quick questions at the most, ideally with multiple choice answers. Alternatively, you can create a poll directly in Facebook on your page or in a group, or you can make a short poll on your Instagram story.

Some survey ideas to generate engagement:

- What is your favorite yoyo shape: O, V, H, W, M?
- How long do you like your string: pocket, belly button, chest, head?
- How many hours a day do you yoyo: <1, 1-2, 2-3, 3-4?
- Which yoyo performance did you like better at the Worlds this year? (list four)
- Favorite non-1a style of a yoyo trick: 2a, 3a, 4a, 5a?
- How do you carry your yoyo: bag, belt clip, pocket, hard case?
- What color would you choose if you had to pick one: blue, black, pink, purple, green?

You can also ask non-yoyo questions and have a little fun.
- Which is your favorite type of music: Country or Western?
- How many pets do you own: 0, 1, 2, 3, I need help
- Are geese the enemy of mankind or just poop machines?

Again, choose a tactic that best fits your brand image and keep the content rolling.

THIRD-PARTY GIVEAWAY MANAGER

If, like me, you are forgetful and have a hard time remembering what's happening and where, a third-party giveaway program is a must. I'm still experimenting with them myself, but there are a few to choose from. I've had some success with Gleam.io and Rafflecopter. A quick search on Google for "Social Media Manager" will pull up several comparisons. Choose one with the best mix of useful options and an affordable price. Also make sure it's a reputable site that will follow the rules. The last thing you want is to lose access to one of your social media platforms because you didn't pay attention to the rules.

How it works

Create an account and follow the steps to create a contest. You can give people multiple ways to enter using different platforms. For example, you can have people view and like a post on Facebook or visit a YouTube channel. If you upgrade to a paid subscription, you can also collect contacts for your mailing list, but that is going to cost you US$30–$50 per month or more. To get around this, I like to use the "comment on a blog post" feature. I can put some product information in the post as well as a link to my mailing list. If you want to be blunt, you can write a blog post that is just a mailing list signup form. Ask them to comment whether they decide to join the list or not. You can also get some pretty good information from people by asking a question about an upcoming release. (What color should I use? What do you think of this logo?)

Every marketing tool can be overused. Remember your 80–20 balance and keep in mind that giveaways are in the 20 percent. You don't ask for a purchase, but you do ask for time and attention. I try to do a giveaway about once a month, twice at the most. If I do more than one giveaway per month, I separate social media platforms (Instagram this week, Facebook the next) instead of blanketing them all. Also, keep in mind that constant giveaways can dilute your sales. You'll find people holding off on purchasing because they know they'll have another chance to win soon.

CHAPTER 8 -

CUSTOMER SERVICE

Every time a customer interacts with your brand is a critical moment. Most businesses are built around repeat customers. You don't want people to buy one yoyo; you want them to buy all the yoyos! Repeat customers take work, but they are worth cultivating.

SHOPPING EXPERIENCE

A simple, attractive, and easy-to-navigate online store comes first. Look at other successful brands for layout suggestions. Your product description includes attractive photos that are well edited. All the necessary specifications are clear and easy to find. The "buy now" button is clear as are the options. The photos are really important. I've had customer complaints because my photos weren't clear enough and the actual color didn't match the photo. Pop on Amazon or eBay and buy a collapsible light box with a couple of good-quality photo lights. You can get away with using your cell phone to take pictures if it's got a decent camera, but getting a tripod for it is helpful. Don't forget that in your product description you can add links to other items in the store as an upsell: "Don't forget to stock up on string."

Keep barriers to the sale as few as possible. That impulse buy needs to happen fast. Have a seamless cart-and-checkout option, including as many payment options as you can manage. PayPal and major credit cards are a must. Make sure to note the fees that you will have to pay for those and build that into your planning and accounting. When you set up your webstore, also remember to set up the sales taxes for the province, state, and country in which you do business.

SHIPPING

Once your customer has made their purchase, the single biggest mistake you can make is slow shipping. I don't know about you, but I will pay more for a product that is going to arrive quickly and cost me less to be shipped. Amazon Prime service is the poster child for that bit of psychology — "free" shipping and an arrival within days. Although you sell a specialty item, a long wait can still put people off.

Research your shipping options. Are bulk rates available through your webstore platform? Is there a third-party service that will save you time and money? Can you cut costs by purchasing your own boxes in bulk?

A shipping service integrated with your webstore is a must. If an order comes in, your store should generate the shipping label and make a postage purchase quick and easy. Once you get up to any kind of decent volume, I can't stress enough how valuable a thermal postage printer is. I got a refurbished one for US$130 and being able to print and peel saved me enough time in the first 2 months that it paid itself off. It's also great for printing labels for my storage bins.

Ongoing Communication

Ongoing communication is important. My system automatically emails the generated tracking number to the customer. I recommend limiting your options to "tracked" and "insured" shipping services. This ensures that you are covered if the package goes missing. It also allows customers to track the package themselves rather than email you every two days. You can offer cheaper, non-tracked options, but keep in mind that if the package doesn't appear in a timely fashion, you will have to refund or replace the package at your cost. I've shipped over one thousand packages to customers over the years, and I can tell you that if they don't hear from you within 48 hours of their order, you will receive an email. If there is going to be a delay, let them know right away.

Also, consider your time. How far do you have to travel to drop off boxes, and does it make sense to pay a courier to deliver them? I did that for a couple years. It was a one-hour round-trip drive to the depot to ship packages. A local courier service picked up my boxes for US$5 and delivered them the same day. Now if I have time, I spend 30 minutes each way on the bus. If I don't, I use a courier.

PROBLEM SOLVING

The old customer service saying "the customer is always right" comes into play here. As a salesperson, your job is to make sure that customers are satisfied with their experience. Keep in mind how much of your business revolves around word-of-mouth advertising. Sometimes, all it takes is one customer getting angry and screaming all over social media to set you back.

I always buy insurance for my packages. Otherwise, it's a gamble. One in every fifty packages may go missing. You can gamble if you'd like, but I prefer to have the safety net.

If a package does go missing, you don't want to make the customer wait for the insurance to pay out. Once you are reasonably sure it's gone and are ready to start arguing with the postal service, either refund or replace the package. Treat the occasional replacement yoyo you give to somebody as a cost of doing business.

In the event of a delay, you also have the option of offering somebody a one-time free shipping code for the next order. It's a small chunk of your profits, but it can make a big difference if you want a return customer.

It's all about creating positive experiences. No matter what happens, your goal is to leave your customer feeling like you did everything in your power to keep their experience positive. You won't always succeed, but if you are willing to make the effort, mistakes can turn into the very thing that builds trust in customers' mind and brings them back again and again.

CHAPTER 9 -

SPONSORSHIP

Trust sells products. There is a reason sports brands pay big dollars to champion athletes to wear the brand logo or sponsor events within their industry. It's a way to put your brand in front of customers who want exactly what you sell. Further, sponsorship allows you to borrow the fame and trust earned by professional players and official events.

SPONSORED PLAYERS

A champion athlete carries a massive fanbase of people who dream of being champions themselves. "If I wear those shoes, I'll be able to jump like that player." "I need that specific hockey stick to be the best." Champions have a level of trust earned through their skill, which is lent to the sponsoring brand. When you sponsor a player who has built up social capital through championship wins or community contribution, you buy the trust they have earned.

Choosing a player to sponsor is difficult. You are essentially taking on an employee (although not in the legal sense). Managing them adds to your workload and costs you money.

David at One Drop Design in Eugene, Oregon, shared his thoughts on choosing a player:

> In our view, a sponsored player is a representative of the company. Who they are as a person is the most important thing. We fully support our players if they want to compete, but winning contests is not our focus. Of course, they need to be good at yoyoing and offer something unique. But if they aren't a cool person, then it's not happening.

Coffin Nachtmahr, owner of Oh-Yes-Yo in Baltimore, has a more casual approach that works with his brand image. One that's less about business and more about an artist helping friends:

> I just wanted to give some unique yoyos to guys who couldn't afford it at that point in time. These guys were so rad, I had to be around them, or just needed a proper support group to push them forward.

So, what does this look like for you as a boutique brand owner? If you recall from my experiences running King Yo Star, I struggled to sell yoyos in the beginning. Once I sponsored a U.S. National Champion (Jake Elliot), King Yo Star became a trusted brand. Retail stores started selling my yoyos, and many more players were willing to buy one. It was a costly gamble though, nearly US$1,500 for a plane ticket to the Worlds to have him on the team for a year. Likely, you are neither willing nor able to make that kind of commitment at the boutique level. I could do it only because the owner of the brand was willing to spend the money. You will also be hard pressed to find a player at that level who isn't already sponsored by a bigger brand.

Should a new boutique brand sponsor players? I will suggest that you move slowly. When I started Rain City Skills, I tried to put together a team right away and ended up with some who weren't a good fit. Think about what you can do yourself and where you find the gaps in your skill set. If you are a champion-level yoyoer producing video and written content, you may be able to self-promote in the beginning. If you are a quiet introvert who likes to make yoyos but hates talking to people, you need to find a few people to put a public face on your brand.

Reasons to Sponsor Players

Sponsored players are a great way to get your brand name out there. They offer a fanbase as well as being busy and active online. You can't be everywhere at all times, so it's nice to have other people out there for you. It also puts a filter between your brand and the customers that is more palatable and less pushy. A sponsored player on your team can offer one of your brand's yoyos when somebody asks for recommendations, which is, of course, a type of promotion — just not as obvious as self-promotion.

You may not be able to afford a National or World Championship contender, but there are plenty of up-and-coming players who are starting to rank in regional contests. There is a large market of younger players looking for competition yoyos. They tend to pick based on brand names and on players they wish to emulate. Even if your players aren't ranking top three but are interesting to watch, their contest videos are still good advertising. Odds are pretty good that they're also going to be able to put out a semi-regular trick circle or trick collection videos.

If you can get a player that fits one of the many niche groups that you don't fit into, that gives you more reach. Don't want to spend your days on social media? Find four players on your team. They all have followings on various social media platforms. And find somebody that puts out regular tutorials, reviews, or written blog posts.

I like to bring those people on board who can help work behind the scenes — players who can fill in some of the gaps in my skill set and who can engage with different aspects of the hobby. This works because I'm clear about expectations on both sides and am constantly checking in to make sure the exchange works in both directions. This also works because I'm not currently operating in the competition yoyo market. The majority of my sales are based around "that's really cool!" So my players fit that image.

Challenges with Sponsoring Players

There are some downsides to having a team of sponsored players promoting your brand. The first one people would think of is cost. If you sponsor a competitor, you are likely to pay registration fees, if not hotel and travel as well. That's a lot of cash out of your pocket if you're a small or boutique brand. At the very least, you give them yoyos out of every run that you release. Those yoyos can eat up your profit margin in a hurry if you have a big team and slow sales.

I have tried a number of different strategies to choose players, with limited success. I like meeting people at contests and finding someone who gives off the "I'm really dedicated to yoyos" vibe. I've tried what was basically a job interview format — Google Form with a range of questions, then a shortlist of interviews that was not so successful.

The problem is that there are so many good yoyoers that it's hard to choose who will represent the brand in the best way. I hate the idea of sponsoring someone and then essentially firing them if they don't fit as well as I would've liked. I had a player who joined the team and then realized very shortly that life was getting way too busy to hold up their end of the commitment. They were completely understanding and fine with our parting ways. However, I do dread the idea of having someone leave the team when they're upset or angry about it.

Remember that when you sponsor a player, they are a face of your brand and that everything they do online then becomes associated with you. Years ago, I remember seeing a player who made some publicly unethical decisions. The brand owner who sponsored him had to deal with the fallout, made the decision to remove this player from their team, and publicly apologized for this person's behavior. A sponsored player is part of your brand's story. Spend some time poking through their public persona and making sure they're going to be a good fit.

Agreements

There are many ways to come up with agreements with your players. Every brand I have talked to has had a different system. Here are a few different options that I have come across.

- Discounted Yoyos. I've seen this one a couple of times. Players are expected to buy their own yoyos, but they get a discount.
- Yoyos in exchange for activity. This can be very well scripted, or it can be very loose and flexible.
- Travel expenses and registration fees.
- Paid employees. That's far less likely at the boutique level. That does happen higher up.

Keep in mind you will need to supervise players to make sure they stick to the terms. Don't wait 6 months then get angry they weren't doing what you expected. Communicate often and make expectations clear. Renegotiate as needed.

How to Choose Players

Finding the right players is going to be time consuming and can be expensive. Start with your social circle within the yoyo world. Is there anyone you know who will passionately get on board and be a good rep for your team? Scour Instagram under the hashtag #trickcircle and see who stands out as innovative and interesting. If you look for competition players, look at state and regional contest rankings and find the top-ranked, non-sponsored players. Look at long-term investment and try to find an up-and-coming champion. If you are friends with high-level players, see whether they know anyone who isn't sponsored but should be.

During this process, you are going to end up giving away some yoyos to players who won't accept the sponsorship offer. Needless to say, you won't get those yoyos back. I've had this happen a few times, and it felt a little like they were just trying to score some free yoyos. Well, that's part of the cost of the business. A player on the way up is going to be looking for the best fit. Maybe I didn't offer them enough. Remember that when you start out you are small fish in a big pond.

The only hard and fast rule I'll give you for choosing players for your team is **move slowly and carefully**. Don't jump in and build a huge "team" right away. Choose your players with care and lay out the rules ahead of time, in writing. You can always make changes later, but start out with careful consideration.

EVENT SPONSORSHIP

Look at stadiums, competitions, conventions, and any event that draws large numbers of people. Corporate logos are everywhere.

Contests are an anchor point of the yoyo world. We mark our calendars with the ones closest to us and often try to find a way to get to the bigger ones. In any industry, a visible logo at contests or trade shows builds trust and attracts customers.

I've run yoyo contests for nearly a decade. Contests run on sponsor dollars. I can tell you that those dollars used to be easier to find. There were a dozen brands I could hit up every year with success. Now, there are a handful of big brands that are overstretched, dozens of small brands, and an ever-changing wave of boutique brands. Something for us all to keep in mind is that starting up boutique brands splits up the market. The sponsorship dollars aren't concentrated in a few big brands to be doled out to all the contests. It is my personal opinion that we have an obligation to help the sport grow by supporting contests.

What does it cost?

How will you decide what contests to support? The cost for a contest usually starts at around US$100 in either cash or product. From the contest organizers' perspective, cash is always better than product. They have bills to pay and want to offer champions a cash prize. If you donate product, they need to either raffle it off or sell it, adding to their workload.

For you, as a sponsor, contests are a good way to use some leftover yoyos from a previous run that aren't selling to buy yourself some advertising. Organizers do need prizes for the event, but I like to try to offer at least a bit of cash. Even if it's only $20 with a couple yoyos, it helps.

What do you get?

In exchange for sponsoring an event, you usually get a tiered set of benefits, depending on how much you pay. Here is a list of a few:

- Your logo on the event website and Facebook page
- Words of thanks by the MC during the event
- Your logo on the stage backdrop
- Your logo on printed material — schedules, score sheets, flyers
- A vendor table
- Free registration for you or one of your players
- Logo in the official videos

How valuable is contest sponsorship? Is your logo on a banner for one day worth $100? Is having my logo at the beginning of videos worth $200? Is this bit of advertising going to result in enough sales to offset the cost?

These are the wrong questions. Sponsoring an event is not about direct return on investment. It is about engagement and growing your brand's story. When you sponsor contests, your brand is associated with community involvement. You're seen as somebody helping move the sport forward rather than just taking money out of it. That logo on a banner or a video won't send most viewers digitally dashing to your website to buy yoyos, but it's one of those many ways your brand becomes safe and familiar. Enough of those and you've got a new fan. Marketing is a long-term investment.

What contests should I sponsor?

When it comes to choosing where to put your very limited sponsorship dollars, I would suggest you start with the nearest contest you can get to. If you can show up in person and run a table, you're going to get face-to-face connections. If you can put a yoyo in hands for people to try, they will be more likely to buy later. The next best thing is to sponsor a contest one of your sponsored players can attend.

If you're not able to attend contests at all, then your dollars are best spent on the biggest contest you can afford. The key thing here is to plan ahead rather than respond to the first person that asks you for a donation.

The Boutique Yoyo Collective

There is one other option to get your name into bigger contests: The Boutique Yoyo Collective (BYC). In 2013, I attended the World Yoyo Championship in Prague. I was really excited to be traveling to another continent to check out some brands that we can't get in North America. I was quite disappointed to find the big brands that you can get in any online store. I learned that this was because of the prohibitive cost of sponsoring Worlds.

To that end, I have put together the BYC. We are a group of boutique and small brands that all pitch in together to sponsor bigger contests and have a chance to share our products at a table. My plan is to grow this into an organization that helps spread the sponsor dollars around to the smaller contests. We successfully ran tables at the 2018 USA National contest and the 2019 World Yoyo Contest and are looking forward to the future!

Sponsorship management is a challenge. It's a part of the job of running a yoyo business than can make it feel like work. It can also be an incredibly rewarding part of the job. If you sponsor a competitor, you get to share the joy in their wins. When your trick innovator receives high praise for an amazing trick video, you know you helped encourage that success. When you see people gushing online about how much they enjoyed a contest, you get to enjoy the feeling of having made it happen. I wouldn't be where I am now if I hadn't been on team MonkeyfingeR. That opportunity pushed me to move from yoyoing as a casual hobby to yoyoing as a passion and a business. If you can offer that to someone, they will help you drive your business to success.

CHAPTER 10- PAID ADVERTISING

This is a difficult topic. It can be challenging to justify spending your limited funds on advertising when you've just gambled your (or someone else's) savings on a run of yoyos. But the old adage of "you need to spend money to make money" holds true.

Advertising is an art. Creating an advertisement that will generate sales even more so. Unless you are targeting non-yoyoers with the hopes of selling them their first yoyo, you are looking at a very small market. If you are careful with your social media marketing strategies, you can find a lot of your customers organically.

Ads can extend the reach of your content posts, build your mailing list or notify long-time customers about a release. The platforms you are working with limit how much of your audience sees your content, and the only surefire way around that is to pay to have your message pushed out.

Paid advertising is available on most platforms and is generally easy to use at a basic level. It's also very challenging to get a good return on investment (ROI) out of. Fifty dollars in ads to get one sale is a quick recipe for bankruptcy. My experience and knowledge on the topic are thin, and, as such, the specifics of how to create and run successful ads are outside the scope of this book. The actual mechanics of creating and running ads changes all the time. I recommend finding the most recent guide on YouTube and watching that to get you started. The following section offers a synopsis of how ads work on each of the platforms you are likely to work with.

GOOGLE

When you set up a Google ad, you buy a word or phrase. The first two-three responses in a Google search are paid ads. Whoever spends the most, gets those spots. Anyone who clicks on those ads is taken straight to a page on your website, and you pay for that click. How much you pay depends on how popular that word is. I imagine that trying to buy an ad for the title of a Disney movie would be rather expensive. But what it does let you do is target people who actively look for yoyos.

You can also use these ads to test out branding ideas. The name of your yoyo or brand can affect your sales. You can test that by putting up an ad for that name that just leads to an information page about your brand or a pre-order for the yoyo. The point is simply to be able to track how many people will click on that ad. If you try three or four different names, you'll get an idea for which one works the best.

YOUTUBE

YouTube ads are run through Google ads. They are also very complex. If you've spent any time on YouTube, you've seen a variety of ads. Some start at the beginning of the video; others interrupt longer videos. They usually run for four or five seconds before you can skip them. Advertisers pay only if a viewer watches thirty seconds of the ad. Sometimes, one doesn't have the option of skipping. Those ads are billed at total time viewed and can be more costly.

If you decide to dive into YouTube ads, watch some tutorials and really be careful about your spending. Craft clear and to-the-point videos that get your message across in a short period, without a lot of reading.

FACEBOOK AND INSTAGRAM

Since Facebook owns Instagram and has integrated the two, I'm going to talk about them together. Instagram ads can be created and controlled from your Facebook account. This involves switching your Instagram account to a business account in the settings.

Facebook posts on your business page or timeline do not go very far. I've read that as low as 2 per cent of your followers see the posts organically. Generally, the only people to see them are the ones who interact with your content on a daily basis or specifically check your business page. To get your content far and wide you have two paid options.

The first is a ***boosted post.*** When you have a successful post, Facebook will send you a notification asking whether you want to "boost" the post. They will then push it out to a wider group. I haven't seen much value in this. Generally, if I've had a post that's been successful enough to get 200 views on its own, the content has done the work for me. Spending US$20 to have another three hundred people see it doesn't make sense.

The other option is a ***paid ad.*** These are different from boosted posts because you specifically create these to achieve a goal. You have more control over who sees your ad, what they see, and what they do when they interact with it. Target your ad based on location demographic and profile information. You can also target by interest, and, most importantly, you can target your existing audience.

This last one is the most potentially useful option. A customer's liking a business page doesn't mean they see your posts. Use a paid ad to target the people who like your page. If you make your way into the ads manager you can create audiences based on individuals who interacted with a post (that contest you ran that got 600 likes) or the names on your mailing list. You can even extend it to the friends of those people, which is a great way to widen your audience to people who are likely interested in what you sell. Finally, Facebook can generate "look-alike" audiences of people who are similar to those who are already fans. Use caution if you decide to explore Facebook ads. Keep your daily spend low and experiment for a while until you find a format and audience that gets you result. Treat this like a trip to a casino, don't spend any money you can't afford to lose.

OFFLINE

What about the local newspaper? Flyers? Posters? Business cards? You'll find a host of more traditional marketing options available. If you opt to make a budget-friendly beginner yoyo, you may want to spend some money marketing locally. Newspaper ads may work, although I've never tried them. I suspect the cost is too high for the potential return. Flyers or posters on poster boards near schools or recreation centers may work. If you go this route, my best recommendation is to talk to schools. If you offer a profit share, they may be willing to have you come in and do a demo, and then send a notice home to collect orders. Many people have made a good living doing school yoyo shows and workshops.

My best recommendation for offline spending is business cards and stickers. They can be included with your online sales as further promotion, and if you are like me, you usually have a yoyo with you when you are out in public. You want to have something to hand to someone who is watching in awe as you flawlessly execute a Rock the Baby trick. You never know, they may become your biggest fan!

Advertising is tricky; paid advertising is even more so. It can be an extremely powerful tool; the fact that the whole industry exists to create advertising backs that. It can also be a black hole your money falls into. Be cautious and take the time to read blogs, read books, listen to podcasts, and learn as much as you can, and I'm sure you'll find ways to boost your sale.

CHAPTER 11 -

DISCOUNTS AND FREE

GIFTS

One of the keys to a successful business is training your customers to pay a full price for your goods. This isn't a firm rule. There are plenty of businesses that operate around a steady stream of discounts and sales. There is a craft store chain in North America that does this. Everything in the store is brutally overpriced. But they always have a "50% off your first item" sale going. I suspect they make their money off people not wanting to make a trip the next day for the second item at 50 per cent off, who instead pay the full price. I can't see this working with yoyos.

A discount code can be a useful tool to generate sales a couple times each year. It can also be the first step on a slippery slope to a failed business. If you offer a percentage discount on a very rare occasion (like Black Friday), you'll generate some extra sales and clear out old inventory. If you offer a discount every month, your customers will stop paying retail and will wait for the next discount. It will feel like your product is not worth paying full value for, since if they are patient they can get it cheaper. This is especially bad if you sell your yoyos through an online store because you're undercutting their prices. That's not to say don't do it at all. Just be aware of the consequences of overusing this strategy. You want to train your customers to pay a full price.

DISCOUNT CODES

Targeted discount codes are a great way to thank your most dedicated customers, re-engage old customers, or deal with customer service issues. Delay in shipping? Free shipping on your next order. Product arrived damaged? Offer a replacement or a code of 40% off for the next order. I've had this work a few times. The customer kept the damaged product and then made another purchase. I lost profit on the second purchase but made two sales instead of one and didn't have to cover the costs of shipping out a replacement and shipping back the damaged yoyo. I used this same tactic a couple times when I accidentally shipped the wrong yoyo to a customer.

I use a service that integrates with Shopify, which is a points system. Customers earn points when they first subscribe by "following" me on social media. After that, they earn points on their purchases that they can use to get free shipping or a dollar value discount. This kind of thing is hard to manage yourself, but with an automated system it's quite simple. Not all my customers use it, and I suspect the pop-up annoys an occasional customer, but the bargain hunters will be more likely to follow through on a purchase, knowing it'll lead to a discount next time.

Another option is the buy-one-get-one deal. Again, this one should be used only sparingly. If you have a handful of last year's model left over, your discount could be "Buy a Duckhat yoyo priced $50 or higher and receive a Duckhat Webfoot for 50% off!" Make it a specific discount and not a "50% off your entire order" or you'll end up selling your latest release at a discount as well. This type of inventory-clearing discount will also help customers make the decision to buy your newest release: "I'm paying for shipping on the discounted item anyway; might as well include a second yoyo now and save the future shipping cost." As I said before, people hate paying for shipping.

A site-wide discount should be used sparingly. Many stores offer such on major shopping holidays. For example, a 10%–20% discount on Black Friday is common. It drives increased sales on that day but also trains your customers not to shop during the first half of November in anticipation of the sale. On the other hand, the sale DOES have the benefit of making your products appeal to potential new customers. No sale at all on Black Friday also means missing out on a lot of dollars spent in other stores.

NON-YOYO GOODS

A free sample has long been a successful advertising tool. Obviously, it's not viable to give away samples of your yoyo, but you don't need to. Remember that you aren't selling yoyos — you are selling your brand. Yoyos happen to be your main product, but anything that reminds people of your brand has value. Non-yoyo goods often included with shipped-out orders are referred to as "extras." They can also be free items given away as part of a contest or promotion.

Stickers

Stickers are a pretty standard place to start. I order a custom sticker for every yoyo release and include a bundle of them with every yoyo that gets shipped out. The idea is that a new customer buying the latest yoyo may receive a sticker from a previous release and follow their curiosity to the product page. I stick with the least expensive sticker option, which is usually a 2-inch x 2 inch square. I don't create the most insane custom art for my stickers either — often just a variant on my brand logo. If you have art skills or a friend who will do some drawings in exchange for a yoyo, you may go with higher quality/custom design stickers. I have a graphic designer essentially on retainer. He gets one of every yoyo I make and generates graphics as needed. You can even sell them as a separate product!

Like everything else in this business, the more stickers you buy the cheaper they are. You're probably not going to need ten thousand stickers, but quantities of five hundred to one thousand stickers usually end up costing close to the price of one hundred. Have a look at both online and local physical print shops and find the middle ground between the volume and the price. You can usually get basic stickers for $50–$60, larger or fancier for $100 or so.

Patches, pins, keychains, and more

The next option is patches, pins, keychains, mousepads, and other small goods that can be engraved or embroidered with your logo. Odds are good that there is someone locally that does such work, or you can pop online and look around. If you want large volume, AliExpress (smaller qty.) or Alibaba (larger bulk order) are often your cheapest option. Be prepared for hit-and-miss quality. Print-on-demand services are becoming more common as well. These sites allow you to upload your art and create a product that is printed only when you make a sale. The price per unit is usually higher than if you want one hundred or one thousand of them made all at once, but there is no up-front cost. This sort of item is best used for a limited promotion, or as part of the "extras" packaging with a yoyo. You can also set up a print-on-demand item that you can sell through your online store.

Shirts and other apparel

There is a reason why half of the people walking down the street wear t-shirts, hats, or other articles of clothing with a brand on it. If you can sell someone a shirt with your logo, they essentially pay for the privilege of advertising for you. Pre-ordered large batches of shirts are the cheapest option on the surface but are also the riskiest. If you make thirty shirts, you can usually get them for USD$8-10 each. But how do you decide on the sizes? If you give them away as a promotion, that matters less. But if you are looking at making your money back, you will struggle. You're pretty much guaranteed to sell a few and end up with a bunch that people won't buy. If you're looking at it as a product to make money off of, you'll have to price to account for "dead stock." Even then, your odds of breaking even are not good.

The alternative is print on demand. You don't pay for the shirt until someone orders it. Sites like Teespring and Printful will print and ship directly to your customer. If you are looking at t-shirts as a promotional item, they are expensive to give away. But if you price them at cost, they're cheap enough for an impulse buy.

FREE CONTENT

Aside from physical goods, you also have intellectual property you can use. You have picked up many skills in your life by this point. I'm an elementary school teacher, which means I'm a generalist. When I was a substitute teacher, I had to be prepared to teach anything from Kindergarten shoe-tying to Grade 12 AP Physics. The trick was to be able to look through the materials in the ten minutes before class and gain just enough knowledge to be able to deliver the lesson that day. Mix in an ability to artfully redirect questions to someone more expert (in the Physics class, that would be literally any of the students), and you are a teacher!

One of the fundamental facts of teaching is that you just need to know more than the person you're teaching. If all you can do is the first ten yoyo tricks, you can teach those to somebody that knows only five of them. Share your knowledge, even if it's going to appeal to beginners only. Try filming some tutorials teaching tricks while wearing your brand t-shirt and using your brand yoyo. Start with easy tricks. There are dozens of YouTube videos teaching beginners to wind a yoyo, but yours will still get views. Some of those viewers will see your logo and wonder what else you have to offer.

Don't be afraid of offering your understanding and knowledge of skills that surround yoyo. If you are good at editing videos, make a little video walking people through some tips and tricks of using your favorite piece of editing software. Photoshop? Audio editing? Recording? Make a video explaining it, put it on your website, and share it. Title it "Audio editing for yoyo competitors" and make your tutorial about cutting together a three-minute edit for your yoyo routine. An educational blog is also free content to give away and a good way to direct traffic to your website. Anything you can do to get your message out and to show that you add to the community helps you out.

The effective use of discounts and free goods is a balancing act. Everything has a cost, and you can easily spend far more than you earn. On the other hand, the long-term benefit of spreading brand awareness is part of your equation. As with everything marketing related, start where you are comfortable and figure out what you can add to help you stand out.

PART III - MAKING AND SELLING YOYOS

CHAPTER 12 - YOYO DESIGN CASE STUDY: THE DUCC

The Yoyo design process is a blend of both science and art, mixing aesthetics and function. I am not a yoyo designer. I'm an ideator. My skills revolve around generating ideas and building a story. When planning a yoyo release for Rain City Skills, I work rather backwards. I first decide what idea I want to sell and start building the story. Then I narrow down a type of yoyo that will fit that idea. Then I connect with an experienced designer to turn that idea into a quality design. Part of success in business is knowing your strengths and knowing when to hire experts.

This section begins with the creation of a design and interviews with experienced yoyo designers. From there, we move into finding a shop and getting your yoyos made. I conclude with strategies for selling them, so you can move onto the next design.

For starters, I want to share a project from the beginning of 2018. This case study demonstrates the process of design, testing, and production, as well as some of the pitfalls to avoid.

DESIGN BY COMMITTEE

I decided to organize a community yoyo design with the Facebook group "Yoyo BST & Talk." Devin Flores (A yoyo designer) offered to help out by creating the actual design schematics. We started with broad specifications and narrowed down to the small details. Each step involved a survey of the community, basing the next aspect of the design on that information — a total of twelve design questions listed below. In the end, we had a yoyo design.

Then I ordered a batch of prototypes. I decided to work with the company Magic Yoyo to machine the parts, as they are affordable. Prototypes are usually ordered in very small batches (four-five pieces) and cost far more than the full production run does. On average, I usually pay US$250–$300 — about US$60 per yoyo. But this yoyo was different. Over one hundred people helped design it, so I decided to invite them to test it as well and took pre-orders for prototypes.

We ended up with more orders than I expected and quickly reached the point where it was cheaper to make a hundred yoyos. Everyone understood that they were gambling and that the yoyo would likely have flaws. That is why you prototype your design after all.

I ordered the yoyos and waited. As soon as they arrived, I shipped them out to everybody who pre-ordered and then put the rest up for sale. I was very, very clear that they were prototypes and had flaws. I then send out a form with some key questions for feedback. And boy, was there ever feedback!

TESTING A PROTOTYPE

This design had more flaws than any prototype I'd ever made. In hindsight, that shouldn't have been a surprise, considering how experimental the design process was.

There were 2 major flaws to consider. If you are a non-yoyoer reading this, forgive the jargon. I've provided a diagram in appendix A to assist with part names. The recess for the response pads was too shallow, so the pad stuck out a little bit. The gap was a little too thin to start with, so the response pads dragged against the string and cut down spin time. The thumb grind lip came out razor sharp. This had the double effect of being hard on the hand as well as having an easily damaged edge.

In the end, the prototype was not the best yoyo, but it was fun to play with, and everybody enjoyed it because they'd been part of the process. It's a testament to how important engaging with the community you try to sell to is. I took all the feedback and put it into a re-designed yoyo. This time, I ordered the usual batch of a half a dozen prototypes to double check whether our changes improved the design. To my great relief, they did! I released another batch of a hundred of them.

It was a bit of a crazy process that I wouldn't recommend to anyone. It required a lot of time on my part and on that of the designer I was working with. It didn't make me any real profit, but it did pay off in other ways. I ended up with a much stronger presence in the community and a handful of new and dedicated fans.

THE QUESTIONS

Here is an outline of the questions I asked the community to vote on. Each step informed the next. I would put a poll up for two days, then hand the results to Devon Flores to come up with some "renderings" or computer-generated images of the design. Then I'd pose the next question, gather results, and he'd use the chosen design to start adding details. Here are the questions I asked, having decided to use 6061 aluminum to keep the product as affordable as possible:

Question 1: General Shape (O, V, H, or W). This was a starting point, with each of these broad shapes having a huge number of potential variations. The result was close, with 38.5 per cent in favor of an H shape. The next closest option (O shape) had the support of 30.4 per cent.
(See appendix A for examples of the general shape options).

Question 2: Ballpark specifications. For each of the three choices, I offered four options in 2 mm increments: diameter range (50–58 mm), weight range (58–68 g), and width range (38–48 mm). These needed to be rough, as later design decisions would affect the final specifications.

The result was 54–56 mm diameter, 64–66 g weight, and 44–46 mm width.

Question 3: Hub design. We were choosing among fingerspin friendly, Lego compatible, and rounded bump or spike. Lego was the clear winner.

Question 4: Gap design. We offered four computer-generated options as the shape of the gap. The one close was actually closer to a "W" shape than the "H" shape we initially chose, but the design would be refined back towards the "H".

Question 5: Inner thumb grind lip (Yes or No). They chose to have a lip.

Question 6: Wall height (distance from the outside of the response pad to the point where the yoyo curves outward). The vote was overwhelmingly for a low wall.

Question 7: Since we chose a Lego hub, I provided some options for what logo I'd include. They chose a Lego head and a small rocket engine. This was the only step where I disregarded the poll. Once the name was chosen, I tracked down some yellow 1x1 blocks with an eye on them that resembled a duck eye.

Question 8: Accessories case. This question was a filler while I waited for the designer to generate examples for the next question. Still, it was an important question, since Rain City Skills is all about the extras. We settled on a fluffy duck zip-up coin pouch.

Question 9: Refined gap design. This step was more about the aesthetics of the gap design. Four choices with a similar overall shape but with some detailed "cuts" (shallow grooves) were proposed to change the look.

Question 10: Sticker Design. I put a call out for artwork. Then, we voted on which drawing to use.

Question 11: Cup Design. We offered three design options. This was the part of the design, which had the most room for variation, and we could have spent weeks on it.

Question 12: Laser engraving. I called out for artwork and then offered five options for voting. We actually ended up with a different logo, and as I look back, I can't remember how. I think someone submitted a design after the fact, and everyone loved it.

Those were the main survey questions I ran through Google drive. I also did a less formal survey directly in the Facebook group to decide on the name and on the spot where the engraving would be placed on the yoyo.

The whole process could have gone on for a lot longer. In the end, I ended up walking the fine line between having (1) enough community involvement and (2) fatigue from reading and analyzing too many survey posts. I still had a skilled designer generate renderings for me (3D pictures of the yoyo based on the drawings). Overall, it was a very successful project, and I'm glad I undertook it.

CHAPTER 13 - THE ART OF MAKING YOYOS

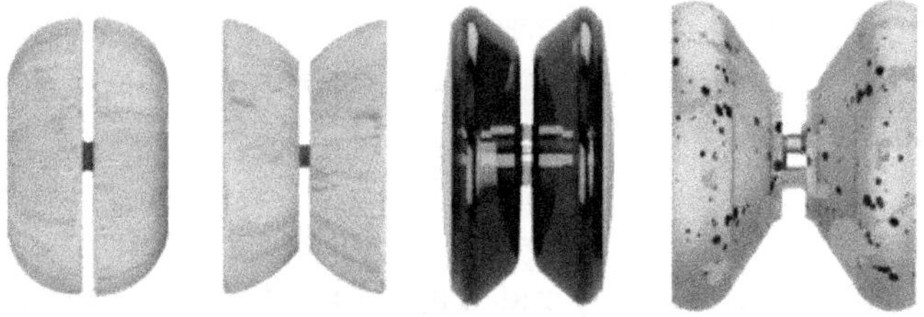

The evolution of yoyo design. Wood to plastic to Aluminum.
The classic "imperial" shape making way for the "wing
shape. The plastic transaxle replacing the wood axle, only to
supplanted by the ball bearing.

Keywords

Machining — Using a machine to carve metal yoyo parts

"CNC" or *"Computer Numerical Control"* — A computer controlling the machining

"Mold" — A hollow container that hot liquid material is poured into and cooled to form an object.

"Injection molding" — A process where plastic beads are melted, forced into a mold, and then cooled to form an object.

"Density" — Amount of material packed into a space (Picture a box of feathers and a box of sand. The sand is heavier because it's packed more densely than the feathers.)

"Alloy" — Two or more materials blended together to make a new unique material (Bronze is an alloy created by blending copper and tin.)

"Tolerances" — The degree of error allowed in a manufactured product

"Vibe or vibration" — A yoyo term referring to the amount of noticeable imbalance in a yoyo

"B-grade" — A yoyo that is in some way below par usually due to machining imbalance, damage, or flaws in the finish.

"Anodizing" — An electrolytic process whereby a protective layer is added to a metal that can be used to add decorative coloring.

"Loss Leader" — A product priced at or below cost designed to draw people into your store in the hopes that they buy additional items (Newspapers in gas stations are generally loss leaders. Odds are good that you will come in to get a newspaper and grab a coffee and muffin as well.)

"A Run of Yoyos" — A batch created at a single time, ranging from a prototype run of four or five to hundreds or thousands (There can be small differences between runs of yoyos due either to design changes or machine tooling differences.)

By this point, you have your branding and marketing machine ready and are probably itching to get to the fun part — creating a yoyo!

Earlier in the book, I mentioned the importance of choosing a product that fits a need in the market. Making a yoyo that is your dream may be fun, but if it doesn't offer anything new, different, or interesting, it won't sell. As you create your design, look around at what is selling and what people are asking for.

Build a team

Your personal skill set will define what you can do yourself and what tasks you need to outsource. My skills lean towards the marketing and customer interaction side of the business. I love coming up with ideas that are fun and exciting and then sharing them with people. To that end, I partner and outsource the jobs I either can't or don't want to do. I run my brand with the goal of being successful enough to provide a small supplemental income. I temper the money goal with a "fun first" policy. If I'm not enjoying what I'm doing, I'm doing it wrong.

I have worked with a few different designers, but the majority of the Rain City Skills products are drawn up by Justin Scott Larson. He is an experienced designer who works in the aircraft industry and designs toys for fun. I connected with Justin when I was trying to design my first set of Begleri. I caught his attention with a series of "What if we do this weird thing with a design?" He'd usually start with a "That's impossible!" reply only to actually make it work twenty minute later. He's as much an artist as a technician, and I value his experience. I've continued to throw him vague and ill-defined ideas for yoyos that should be terrible. But he works his magic and turns them into fun and functional designs. He's worth every handful of peanuts I pay him!

I usually give him a description of what general yoyo shape I want, its weight and dimensions, and some of the distinguishing features. Sometimes, I'll give examples of other yoyos with similar features, or I'll do a rough sketch. Justin will come back with a draft, and I'll offer thoughts on what to change or tweak. This back-and-forth may last a while, or it may be short and sweet. After more than a dozen of designs together, I know I can trust him to figure out what I'm trying to do and turn it into a viable yoyo design.

Graphic design is another area where I'm weak. I could put in the hours to learn Photoshop, but why? I find it incredibly frustrating. I'm not at all interested in learning that skill. I would rather put my time into selling yoyos. It's a math decision — (1) spend four hours of my time trying to get something done or (2) give it to a professional and have it back in 20 minutes. How much am I really going to save doing it myself? Could I earn more than spend in those four hours? So I get others to do my graphic design work for me, and I compensate them in various ways. In some cases, it's a labor trade — I offer some area of my expertise for theirs. Other times, I'm able to trade yoyos for services. There are also times when I spend the money. Graphics and photography are the first thing new customers see, so they are worth being done right.

Your decisions through the design process will reflect the balance between money and time. You spend both now in the hopes of a return later. If this is your first yoyo, it will likely be much later. Your first release will likely be a loss leader — something you put out there to get attention and establish yourself. I still have a dozen of my first yoyo releases sitting on the shelf. That's normal in business. You have to start somewhere.

Here are a few realities to keep in mind, moving forward:

1. It's going to cost more than you expect.
2. It's going to take longer than you expect.
3. Everything that can go wrong will go wrong.
4. It will take longer to sell than you hope.
5. The more you buy the cheaper they get.
6. When it's done, it'll be awesome.

MATERIAL CHOICES

Designing a modern yoyo is a complex undertaking that begins with material choice. Each option has different attributes that guide your design. A design that would be durable if made from titanium might be so fragile as to be useless when made of aluminum. A design optimized for Delrin or Polycarbonate will be unnecessarily bulky when used on 7075 Aluminum. If this is your first time designing a yoyo, I recommend consulting someone who has a strong handle on the physics and math involved.

I asked Justin Scott Larson to share some general thoughts on yoyo design:

> When designing a yoyo, you need to take different factors into play — how it feels in the hand, its appearance, and most importantly, how it will feel when it's spinning during tricks. Choice of metal changes your options for designing the body. Not all aluminum is the same; a different "grade" can be denser. This density allows you to make parts of the yoyo thinner, so you can choose exactly where the weight will sit.

The difference between a good yoyo and an amazing one can be as simple as 0.2 g (.07oz) of weight in just the right place. Titanium allows you to push that envelope even farther, as you can machine titanium to such thinness that if it were aluminum it would allow you to fold it in half.

Here is a short list of the more common yoyo material options:

Wood

- Too many choices to list – depends on the desired outcome

Metal

- aluminum (6061, 7075, 7068)
- titanium
- stainless steel
- brass
- magnesium

Plastic

- POM (trade name Delrin)
- polycarbonate (machined)
- polycarbonate (injection-molded)
- ABS (acrylonitrile butadiene styrene)
- 3D printed plastics

Each of these materials has a different density, will work differently when turned into a yoyo, and will feel different in the hand. Some are easier to machine with precision than others. Density indicates weight and to some degree durability. Determining strength of materials is more complicated than that. The science of metallurgy is well beyond the scope of this book, but I'll provide a brief overview of my understanding from a layman's perspective. Most of my information comes from discussions with machinists, designers, and Internet research.

Wood

A wooden yoyo is the most widely recognized version of the toy. Wood is challenging to work with. Metals and plastics are unlikely to hold critical flaws in the raw material. Wood can. It's hard to tell what you will get when working with wood until you start cutting into it. In the current market, wood yoyos tend to be boutique level throws hand carved on a lathe. It is possible to get them mass produced overseas, but quality control is a big challenge. I bought five hundred cheap ones with my logo on them to use as business cards. Over one hundred were complete garbage, about three hundred required time and attention to get them up to quality, and the rest were good enough to sell.

Wood design options start with the traditional fixed axle design. The easiest option is a three-piece design (two halves and a piece of dowel connecting them). It is possible to carve a yoyo out of a single piece of wood, but it is more difficult.

You can also make a ball bearing wooden yoyo. These require a metal axle and bearing seat assembly. The bearing seat is the spot around the axle of the yoyo where the bearing sits. This has to be a precise design, so the inner ring of the bearing touches the yoyo, but the outer ring doesn't. Carving wood thin enough for a proper bearing seat is very difficult, and such a bearing seat will likely crack or break. Instead, most wood yoyo makers use a custom metal piece that snaps into the wood shell and holds the bearing. If you enjoy working with a lathe, wooden yoyos might be the project for you! I've played with some good yoyos made by hand on a small tabletop lathe.

Metal

For the most part, metal yoyos are "machined" on a CNC Lathe (computer controlled). This differs from a standard lathe in that the entire process is controlled by a computer. The operator programs in all of the details and then leaves the machine to do the work. In very simplified terms, this usually involves three actions:

- One machine pushes the rod of your material into another machine, which spins it.

- A computer-controlled blade carves one side of the part.
- The part is cut from the rod, flipped around, remounted, and the other side is carved.

Grades of aluminum are identified by a number that references an alloy (two or more base metals mixed). The most commonly used aluminum grade for yoyos is 6061. The number system indicates the material used to create the aluminum alloy. The 6000 series of aluminum is a blend of magnesium and silicon with aluminum. The 7000 series is zinc blended with aluminum and can be more durable than 6000s.

A yoyo made of **7075 aluminum** is likely to escape a drop on concrete with less damage than a yoyo made of **6061 aluminum** that is less expensive and is easier to anodize (the surface finish that adds durability and color). In turn, **7068** is stronger than **7075** but is more brittle (more likely to crack instead of dent).

Titanium is stronger than most aluminum, so you can machine it thinner than aluminum while maintaining durability. The raw material is also significantly more expensive as is the machining cost. The material is difficult and time consuming to cut due to its nature.

You have some unique finish options available with titanium, but again, the cost is higher depending on the shop you work with. One fun selling point of titanium is that you can sell yoyos in their "raw" or unfinished form, as customers like the look and feel. It also creates sparks when you "walk the dog" on concrete! Of course, not everyone does it with a yoyo that sells for $300 or more, but a temptation is always there! I once put out a video "sparking" two titanium yoyos, and it garnered a lot of attention and some angry responses (what a waste!) until I pointed out that they were both prototypes being tested.

Aluminum and **titanium** are the most common metals used in yoyos because they sit in the sweet spot of weight and durability. Brass and steel are most often used as weight rings embedded in your plastic, aluminum, or titanium yoyo (see the Mixed Material section below). A full-sized steel yoyo, even machined as thin as it can go, will be too heavy for most players. But a ring of steel or brass in the right place allows you to add weight without bulk.

Where **brass** and **steel** really shine is in mini yoyos. A yoyo with the diameter of a quarter made out of aluminum is too light to spin for very long. Brass or steel give you more weight where it needs to be for a yoyo to be "stable" on a string.

It's a good idea to ensure that whoever is designing your yoyo understands the properties of each metal. There's no point in spending the extra money on 7068 aluminum if you are going to use a 6061 design that doesn't take advantage of the different properties of the metal.

Plastic

Plastic yoyos have been a staple of the yoyo industry for decades. Plastics are well suited for large-scale mass production, which is why they are what you usually see in dollar stores. You can also use higher-quality plastic for high-end boutique yoyos.

There are three different processes to consider: **CNC machining**, **3d printing**, and **injection molding**. There are many available plastics, but the most commonly used for quality yoyos are **Delrin** (POM), **polycarbonate**, and **ABS**.

Each of the plastics has different attributes. The most obvious difference is that polycarbonate and ABS are available in translucent colors, whereas POM is available in opaque (solid) colors only. Strength, durability, and material density vary among them.

I can't give you an easy "this is better than that" comparison. Polycarbonate is denser than ABS and thus can likely handle damage better, but it may be more likely to crack than chip. The science of plastics is outside of the scope of this book. If you wish to work with them, make sure your designer understands the limitations of each. Ensure that the shop you plan to work with has the experience and the tools. I went through three shops trying to find one that could get the Sk8r right. If I'd been thinking at the beginning, I would have gone straight to the third shop, as they have a catalog of POM yoyos under their own brand.

Working with plastic materials gives you three main options:

1. CNC Lathe

This is the same process you use for creating yoyos out of aluminum or titanium. The machine spins a rod of plastic, and the computer carefully guides the blade to carve one side of the part. The part is then cut off, removed, and remounted, so the machine can carve the other side. If done on well-maintained equipment the process can be incredibly precise. Alternatively, it can be very inconsistent. I've had batches of machined Delrin where up to 95 out of 100 parts were perfect. I've also had a batch where half of them weren't good enough for sale. The difference was research, design, and shop selection.

Because these are machined, the minimum order quantities are similar to metal yoyos. You can have twenty made, but it is usually most cost effective to produce a minimum of one hundred at a time. Higher quantities reduce your per-unit cost significantly, but if you think of making two thousand or more, you may be better off looking at injection molding.

2. Injection Mold

Injection-molded plastics are a different category of production. Where machined plastics are carved out of a solid rod, injection-molded yoyos start out as plastic pellets. These are heated to melting and then pushed into a pre-made "mold" in the shape of your yoyo. The plastic in the mold cools and hardens, and then the part is removed and more plastic is pushed into the mold. It is a much faster process than machining, so it has the benefit of having a much lower per-unit cost - kind of.

This setup has four major challenges.

The Mold — A mold for a yoyo costs many thousands of dollars to make. Once you've made it, you can make minor changes by removing material, but you can't add more. If your design just doesn't work, you are out a lot more than the US$300 or so you would have spent on aluminum prototypes.

Minimum Orders — Most shops have a high minimum order. (I've been quoted a minimum of five hundred yoyos per color, with a total of at least two thousand yoyos per order.) So, you pay a one-time cost for the mold plus a per-unit cost for the yoyos. To recoup your investment, you need to be able to sell thousands of yoyos instead of fifty to one hundred. On the positive side, once you have recouped your mold costs, the per-unit cost is low, so there is more room for profit in the long term.

Quality — The biggest challenge is quality and consistency when it comes to parts. If the shop takes great care and maintains their equipment, each piece will be pretty close to the last one. If they punch them out as fast as they can to meet a low-price point, you will get imbalance and vibe. A 25 per cent B-grade rate on one hundred pieces isn't the end of the world. On two thousand pieces, that's five hundred junk yoyos! I considered making an injection-molded plastic yoyo. Then I did the math and realized I'd need to sell at least five hundred yoyos to recoup the cost of mold and parts. That's not including the other costs of doing business.

Shipping — This one blindsided me. I was quoted US$1,200 to ship two thousand yoyos into Canada — and that's before import duties and taxes (usually about US$.050 per yoyo). It made sense; I usually pay $100 to ship one hundred yoyos. That bumped up the cost per unit significantly.

3. 3D Printing

At time of writing, 3D printed yoyos are possible to make, but they are still more of a novelty/art piece than a mass-produced toy. If you want a precise-enough print to avoid having an unplayable yoyo, you are looking at a dozen or more hours spent printing each yoyo. Your printer and process will be the biggest deciding factor here. The details of 3D printing are outside the scope of this book, but don't expect to pump out a production run of yoyos on your desktop 3D printer.

The biggest hurdle to 3D printing is the time required. Where you can make four to eight aluminum or plastic yoyos in an hour on a CNC machine, it can take ten hours or more to 3D-print one at high quality. Add the time to clean and polish the yoyo, and you have a very high time-cost per unit. Since this is such new technology, it's quite possible that we will see prices drop and quality increase in the next few years. For now it's best used for unique, small-batch products.

No matter which plastic you choose, a metal bearing seat and axle assembly is a must. In the event of an impact on a hard surface, a plastic bearing post will often crack, whereas a metal one won't. You can have some fun with this. When I made the "Sk8r" yoyo out of Delrin, I had custom aluminum hubs made in a couple different colors. I've also seen brands engrave a logo on the aluminum hub.

4. Mixed Material

Finally, we have mixed-material designs. Precise weight distribution is the difference between a fun yoyo and a champion-level throw. If you have a lower-density body with a higher-density material ring, you get a higher ratio of weight where you want it.

Justin Scott Larson explains why you would add a steel ring to an aluminum yoyo:

> *The stainless-steel rim (by its very nature of being a denser material) lets you modify the design of a single-alloy yoyo (aluminum, titanium). Where you would normally have to increase bulk (volume), you can get away with a smaller rim.*
>
> *It is not difficult to design a yoyo; that has been proven over and over again. To design a piece of art is magic though. Everyone has a different opinion when it comes to the best competition yoyo, the most fun yoyo, or the most aesthetically pleasing. It's a balancing act.*

The biggest challenge with this technique is that the act of attaching a second piece of material increases the technical difficulty and the risk of ending up with defective yoyos. The shops that specialize in this process are a lot better than they used to be. You are less likely to have the high rate of B-grades that I had in the King Yo Star days with the Rapid.

THE PHYSICS OF DESIGN

Cameron Blair runs his own brand called RevPunx but also creates designs for others who want to make their dream yoyo. He shares a great analogy in order to explain the fine line designers walk, balancing how long a yoyo will spin when stationary with how well it will move in the 3-D space yoyoers use for tricks:

My two favorite analogies for this are hammers and chairs.

When using a hammer, you have a couple options. You can hold it near the weighted head, which will give you more control over it at the loss of power, whereas if you hold it further down the handle, you increase the distance of the weight from the radius of your swing. This means the weighted head actually travels a longer distance, moving faster, and as a result, creates more kinetic energy.

By chair, I'm referring to a classic office chair. If you spin around with your legs tucked in close to your body, the chair will rotate faster. By stretching your legs out, you will lose speed. With your legs out, you have greater kinetic energy from having weight further outward from the center (remember the hammer). The result will give you a longer spin overall, as it will take longer for the friction of the chair to slow you down.

When designing yoyos, more weight at the rims will give you a longer spin time. But since yoyos are also meant to move on a plane while spinning, a yoyo with too much weight on the rims will not respond to displacement as well as a lighter one.

A yoyo with more weight towards the center will be easier to displace (move around and do tricks), as the kinetic energy is closer to the radius, allowing for more "give" when moving through space at the same time as spinning, but at the cost of spin time.

It gets pretty straightforward to just eyeball different weight distributions and assume how they will affect the yoyo. On occasion, I will program it in my software (currently Autodesk Fusion 360). Then, after I create the drawing in 3D and add in my material to get a proper estimated weight, I splice the design into three vertical pieces. This gives me separate pieces for the guts, the mid-section, and the rim. This tells me where I may want to add or remove weight (by slightly changing the design or making sections thicker/thinner) to find a happy medium.

After I find my desired weight and shapes, I'll usually hold on to the design for at least a couple weeks, allowing me to tweak it and change little details. I also create hyper-realistic renderings to try and get the best idea of what it will look like at different angles, colors, in lighting, *etc.* Then it's off to prototyping. Since all of this is pure estimating, you never truly know exactly how it will play out until you hold a yoyo in your hands.

His last sentence is an important one. You can edit and tweak and make changes to a design until the natural heat death of the universe. But in the end, you have to make the yoyo and hold it in your hands to find out whether your design has crossed the line from good to great or to downright magical.

Once you have chosen a material to work with and are ready to design a yoyo, your skill set defines your next step. If you are an experienced designer with software, you are good to go. If you want to try designing by yourself, don't be afraid to get feedback. Keep in mind as you work that every change you make affects just about everything in your design. Go slowly and pay attention to the details along the way.

If you have a general idea of what you want, you can get away with a sketch of your idea that you then hand off to a machine shop. Many machine shops will also work with you on your design as part of their prototyping package. That was my experience with One Drop when I made the Hipster Highlife. I had a friend do a preliminary design; then, One Drop put their decade of yoyo design experience to work.

THE GUTS

Before you get into the big picture of designing, start with the small details that are mandatory for a high-performing yoyo — the bearing seat, axle, and response. Much of the trial and error in design has been done by makers and molders of the past. Don't waste your time and money trying to figure them out yourself. The easiest thing to do is talk to the shop you are working with. If they are experienced yoyo manufacturers, they might be able to handle the details of your design that are industry standard. If you want to do it yourself, I recommend joining the Facebook group called Yoyo Designers. It's a group full of people that design yoyos for fun. Most of the designs tossed around there never make it off the screen. The group members are good natured and very helpful and can provide you with the following basics:

1. Bearing and bearing seat

This is the most critical measurement of the entire yoyo. In the yoyo industry, we use a lettered system with a "size C" (R188) bearing as the standard, and with "size A" (MR105) or "size D" (MR115) as alternatives often used for beginner plastics or special editions. I released both a C bearing and an A bearing version of the Rain City Skills "Sk8r." The smaller bearing version made sense, as the yoyo is a novelty shape with a retro feel. If you plan on making a competition-friendly yoyo, you will be best off sticking to a "C" bearing.

The bearing seat must be precisely measured to fit the bearing. Too tight, and you damage the yoyo; too loose, and it may not spin properly at all. You also must account for surface treatment. Anodizing involves adding a layer of material to the surface. It's a tiny layer, but it can lead to damage later due to a tight bearing. This measurement requires consultation with both the machine shop and the anodizer you plan to use. If they have worked together in the past, that is ideal.

2. Axle

For the most part, the industry standard is to use a set screw (M4x07). The most common length is 8 mm (0.315 inches), but yoyo designers for fingerspin tricks often use a shorter axle. A longer axle increases the lifespan of your yoyo, as it allows for more threads gripping the axle. This is significant with customers who unscrew to remove knots frequently. They will likely end up wearing out the threading nearest to the opening. This is the single most frequent issue I run into with the elementary school yoyo clubs I run. It's followed closely by the constant need to dodge stray yoyos flying at my head.

I recommend sticking with the standard. Just remember to design a thick enough wall at each end of the axle hole to ensure the axle doesn't poke through to the outside of the yoyo.

3. Response

At time of writing, the most common option is pre-formed silicone stickers. There is a rough standard of a pad with a 19 mm (0.75 inch) outer diameter, but the inner diameter and depth vary. This is a question for the shop you choose to work with. I generally have my yoyos made by a shop that also makes their own brand of yoyos. They tend to supply pads, so I let them tweak my design to fit their pads perfectly. I've also had custom pads made (for the *Gamer*), but the minimum order on that was three thousand pads. I still have a big box of pads on the shelf. I guess I need to make more *Gamers*!

THE SHAPE

There are five very general yoyo shapes: O, V, H, W, M. (See image below)

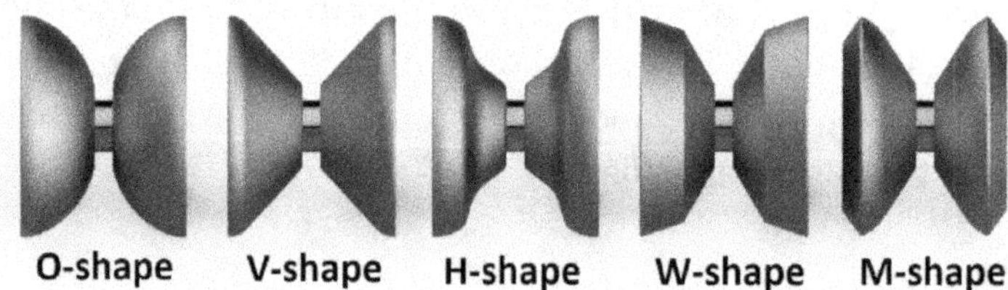

Your first step is to choose one of these broad shapes. Each shape has some benefits as well as drawbacks. The O or "Organic" shape has that clean, classic appeal but is generally the least stable. O-shape yoyos are not usually for competition, but they have a distinct feel to them that many players love. I often see posts on Facebook asking, "What's your favorite O-shape yoyo?" I rarely see that question about any other shape. The V shape is great for horizontal play, as it gives you the largest angled gap. The even distribution of weight is usually best for fast play, skirting the line between stable and easy to move in space. The H shape tends to be more stable but less agile and is often used for 3A yoyos. The W shape is a middle ground between H and V.

Once you have established a basic starting point, you start to look at details. Are you going to stick with the basic shape or start to experiment? Every tiny change you make effects the style and play of the yoyo. This is a place for research (ask your target demographic what they want) and testing (play with as many yoyos as you can). Here is a summary list of the design specifics I used when making the *Ducc* as a reference.

- Width — Standard for a 1a yoyo is 38–48 mm
- Diameter – Standard for a 1a yoyo is 50–58 mm.
- Weight – Standard for a 1a yoyo is 58–68 g
- Hub design – Convex (varies from cylinder to spike); Concave (for fingerspin)
- Gap design – The five main shapes (O, V, H, W, M)
- Bearing size and bearing seat (C – most common; A and D – optional)
- Bearing style (flat, concave, flat center track, groove concave)
- Pad or silicone
- Axle length
- Wall height (from outer edge of the pad to the point where the shape curves off a flat plane)
- Cup design – Thumb grind lip on the rim, ridges, or smooth

You can get only so much out of a drawing. Your next stop is to bite the bullet and order a prototype run.

If I wanted to do the research, I could write an entire book on the physics of designing manufactured spinny things. The best advice I can truly offer is learn as much as you can and then hire someone with the skills and knowledge to take your concept and turn it into a work of art.

CHAPTER 14-

PROTOTYPE

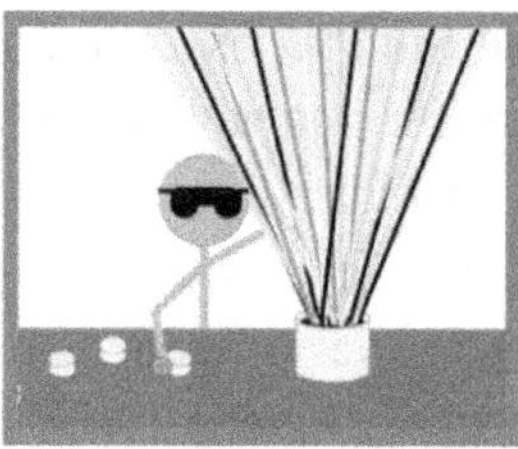

CHOOSING THE RIGHT SHOP

Your success in this business revolves around having a near perfect product — the current yoyo market will tolerate no less. The biggest difference between now and a decade ago is that several machine shops now specialize in yoyo manufacturing. One Drop Design and Foxland Precision are two Made in America options. Both are run by yoyoers who have made and released their own models of yoyo, so they know how detailed their work needs to be.

More options exist overseas. I've worked with the following (in no particular order): FPM, Magic Yoyo, AHAY, TopYo, and YoYo Empire and Vosun. Each of these make their own brand of yoyos as well as manufacture for other companies. I am not going to offer any recommendations here. Just get references and research each shop to decide the best match for your project. Plan to test more than one shop and set your budget to allow for that.

It's All in the Details

It's sometimes possible to find a shop local to you, willing to create a yoyo. But are they able to do the job? The key word here is *tolerances*. When you make a kitchen sink faucet, the exact diameter of the hole the water flows through isn't critical. If one faucet is half a millimeter (0.2 inches) wider than the next, the water still flows. If one half of your yoyo is half a millimeter wider than the next, it is unsellable. Yoyos require far tighter tolerances. A shop that specializes in small machine parts is probably a safer bet than one making industrial-sized machinery. A local shop might be willing to take on the design, but if they don't have the expertise, you may end up throwing money down the drain. That doesn't mean you shouldn't try to shop local — just beware the risks.

Collect Quotes

The cost of your yoyo is determined by many factors, but location is the biggest one. North American machine shops charge more than Chinese ones. That's not surprising, as the cost of running a shop in North America is higher. I'd need to go back to university and do a degree in global economics to be able to give you the full explanation of why. What you need to know is what your targeted customers will buy. If they are going to spend extra to support Made in America, then go for it. If your aim is a lower-price bracket, you may choose overseas. Either way, your next step is to collect quotes.

Shops look at two main factors when generating a prototype quote: (1) material used and (2) machine time. Machine time refers to the entire time the CNC lathe is occupied with your project. This includes programming, loading, cleaning, changing parts, and the time of the operator. If you get five prototypes that take an hour to machine, you might be paying for four hours in total — the amount of time the machine isn't available to make anything else. The quote per piece for a production run will be much lower, because that setup time is amortized over one hundred pieces instead of five.

Different materials have separate base costs. A rod of titanium is more expensive than a rod of aluminum. A larger-diameter rod costs more. Machine time refers to the amount of operation. The computer needs to be programmed. The type of material dictates machining speed. A simple design of aluminum can be mass produced at an average of four to eight yoyos per hour.[1] With titanium you may get two in that time because

---

[1] This is based on numbers provided by multiple shops. A slim yoyo with a very simple design gets you a run of eight; a full-sized yoyo with many complex cuts can give a run of as few as three or four.

titanium is harder to machine. The shop considers these factors combined with the total number you aim to make to give you a price. What you can do is ask the shop to make extra yoyos during the prototyping process. If I've been quoted $300 for a five-piece prototype run, it may be only $100 more for ten pieces.

Shopping for a machinist is like shopping for a new car. You need to look around, ask for references and - if you can - get test samples. You don't just buy the first car you see at the first dealership you find. I have had quotes ranging from $200 to $700 for prototypes of the same design. Sometimes quality and price match; sometimes they don't. Some shops will underprice the prototype in the hopes of gaining your business for a larger quantity later. Others will charge a higher price to give the impression of higher quality (as you might do when you price your yoyos). One key point here is to be willing to spend the money to test a couple different shops. Better to spend an extra $200 now than $3,000 later when you have to redo an entire run.

I've worked with six different shops making yoyos. Some I've been happy with; some less so. One shop that makes exceptional high-end aluminum yoyos was unable to make a passable machined Delrin yoyo for me. Another shop that was able to make the Delrin yoyo had such terrible communication that I couldn't work with them. I've learned that paying a bit more for better communication and customer service is worth it. I like to know that if I order a hundred yoyos and they say that it'll take three to four weeks that I can count on that and plan my promotion around it.

Key Questions

Here are a few good questions to ask:
- References — Do they have previous experience? The shops listed all also manage their own line of yoyos. So you can test their work by buying or borrowing yoyos.
- Testing and assembly — Do they assemble and test for you, or just ship you the parts?
- Quality control — To what degree do they guarantee their work? If there are machining flaws or imbalance in the yoyos, will they give you a refund or credit? What about anodizing flaws?

- Anodizer — What kind of quality does the anodizing shop they work with offer? This is certainly the biggest hurdle for me. I'm currently testing a shop I haven't worked with on a yoyo before. They charged more per part than the competition but have promised me a 90% or higher A-grade rate. Also, if you are going to ask for a complex and specific type of finish, spend the extra to prototype the finish as well.

Price for prototype as well as for fifty, one hundred, or two hundred pieces.

Don't Gamble

Whatever your decision, I recommend always using PayPal Goods and Services for your payment. The protection is worth the added cost, especially when you are gambling thousands of dollars. I can't stress enough: Avoid shops that insist on Western Union, bank transfer, or PayPal "friends and family"! Unless they are willing to ship the finished parts before you send payment, it's too risky. I learned this the hard way — sent $500 to a supplier and got nothing in return.

TESTING

Your testing process depends on what type of yoyo you want to be made and what shop you choose to work with.

1. Structural testing

Walk the dog, throw it up in the air, drop it on all surfaces. Make sure the design will hold up to a beating. You may find you need a longer axle or a slightly thicker rim to keep the yoyo from bending on deforming on impact. Chances are good that a seven-year-old beginner is going to get their hands on one and crank it on the concrete every other throw. This will destroy the surface of the yoyo with dings and scratches and dents, but what you're looking for is how much of a beating it can take before it becomes unplayable. This is especially critical if you are targeting a 4a (offstring) or 5a (counterweight) market (See appendix B).

You also want to take it apart and put it back together a couple of hundred times. Okay I'm kidding (but only partially). You need to know whether the bearing seat is going to be too tight and will strip when it gets unscrewed. This is useful only if your prototypes are anodized in the same way the production run will be. But if they are raw aluminum and the bearing seat is already too tight, then you need to have a talk with your shop.

2. Performance testing

Your sponsored players are where you start testing. If you can, get your throw into the hands of a champion-level competitor for some feedback (off the record if they are sponsored by another brand). Bring it to a club meet or a yoyo contest and get it into as many hands as you can. If you are making a yoyo for a specialized audience like 5A players, make sure some 5A players that are not you get to test it outdoors. Take as long as you need to. You want customers to receive their new yoyo in the mail and hop on social media to say, "This plays amazing!

3. Aesthetic testing

How does it feel? Does it look attractive? These are irrelevant to the yoyo's performance but very important to its sales, especially word of mouth. The Rain City Skills "SETI" is not a performance yoyo. But it looks clean and smooth, and everyone who held it loved the feel in the hand. A lot of my sales with that throw are accompanied by "what a beautiful design" comments. Conversely, I've played with yoyos that are fantastic performance throws, but I wouldn't own one because they were uncomfortable in the hand or unappealing in color. Get your prototypes into as many hands as possible for feedback.

How Many Prototypes Is Enough?

This takes us back to your goal. Are you trying to create the ultimate competition yoyo? Is perfection in design your goal? Then make as many prototypes as that takes. Keep in mind that every prototype you make is going to bump up the retail price of your yoyo significantly. I always order at least one prototype run to test the design. A few times I've gone ahead with the design as-is, usually there are a couple small changes. Twice I've tested prototypes and discovered a catastrophic flaw and been glad I spent the money.

I'll order a second prototype if there are significant changes to be made. I have made as many as five prototype runs on a single yoyo, but that was less about the individual yoyo design and more about trying to find the right shop. I looked at that as more of a long-term investment in the brand. By the time I was done with that yoyo, I had tested four different shops and picked one that hit the sweet spot between price and quality.

What you don't want to do is come up with a design and make hundreds of yoyos without making at least one prototype. I recall one design that a friend made without prototyping. It came out waaaay differently from what they expected. It sold far better than it should have, but I'll call that a lucky accident. I've had a couple of yoyo prototypes that would have been disastrous to have mass produced without testing. In one instance, the bearing seat was too shallow, so the gap for the bearing was too small.

The answer is test as much as you feel you need to within your budget and your design goals.

The prototype process is critical to your success, so don't rush it. Make sure to test the yoyo thoroughly. Don't be afraid to make changes and order a second or third prototype. Also, be prepared to backtrack. I released one yoyo and realized later I should have gone with an earlier version. Multiple prototypes are an added cost, but that investment will pay off in sales. As Justin Scott Larson said, "The difference between good and amazing can be as little as 0.2 g (0.07oz) in the right place." When you finally hit the point where you are happy with your design, it's time to go all in and order a production run.

CHAPTER 15 - THE PRODUCTION RUN

Once you have tested a prototype and are happy with the design, there are three big decisions to make. Quantity, surface finish, and assembly/testing.

The machine shop needs to know what finish they are to add before sending the parts to the anodizing shop. Generally, you choose between a polished finish and a "blasted" finish. "Blasting" involves adding a gentle pitting to the surface with a variation of a technique called a "bead blast." This is generally more popular, as it reduces surface area and thus friction during grind tricks (where you are balancing the still-spinning yoyo on your palm or finger). They also need to know your anodizing plan. Each color you add deposits a tiny layer of material onto the yoyo, which affects how it screws together around the bearing. If the machine shop doesn't account for this, you'll end up with a tight bearing seat that gets damaged every time you take apart the yoyo. This is the quickest way to ruin a perfectly balanced yoyo. A good machine shop will coordinate with anodizing shops to make sure the measurements are right. Alternatives to anodizing are airbrush painting, powder coating, and gold/silver plating. These other options carry the risk of imperfections or increased cost, so they aren't commonly used.

In the U.S., you have to find a separate anodizer. In China, the shop you pick to work with usually handles shipping and negotiations with the anodizing shop. Costs vary, but anodizing in China is cheaper than in the U.S. Of course, cost isn't your only consideration. In my experience, if you choose four colors with Chinese anodizing shops, you will be lucky to get two that match your requirements, and at least one will be drastically different. There's also a higher risk of imperfections. On average, I lose between 25% and 35% to anodizing flaws. These pieces can be sold as B-grades, but it cuts into profit margins. With North American shops, you may get higher consistency but at a much higher cost. Few anodizing shops in North America are set up to do the multicolor finishes many yoyo customers expect.

COLORWAY

The yoyo industry has adopted the textile term "colorway" to describe multicolored yoyos. Most brands try to come up with fun names for colors. Some make up new names every time; others have brand-specific colors, which they use for each release. My colorway names match the theme of each yoyo.

What color is your yoyo going to be? If you plan to order at least one hundred pieces, you'll likely get two or three options, depending on the shop. I've had the same color sell beautifully with one release and badly with the next. If you ask a Facebook group what the best yoyo color is, you'll get a paint store's worth of answers.

Solid Colors

Pink, purple, red, black and gold have sold well for me. Solid-color yoyos are generally less popular than multicolored yoyos, but many do prefer them. An upside to solid colors is the ability to "half-swap." For example, let's say you order three colors: red, black, and purple. You go from three choices to six by offering red/black, red/purple, and black/purple. The biggest benefit of single-color anodizing is the low rate of errors. As soon as you add a second color, you add a second process and then look at a big jump in anodizing flaws.

Laser Engraving

Solid colors are also best for showing off complicated laser engraving art. Chinese shops I've worked with have generally included simple engravings in the cost. You can also get that done locally after you have the yoyos. Be aware that many customers do not like engravings, so leaving some of your run unengraved allows you to appeal to those customers as well.

Splash, Fade, and Acid Wash

"Splash" — The color looks like it's painted on by flicking a heavily laden paintbrush at the yoyo. Stripes of one or more colors added to the base color.

"Fade" — Looks like one half was dipped in one color and another half dipped in the other, with the colors blending on the boarder. I've seen up to a four-color fade. This technique provides you with a high B-grade rate.

"Acid Wash" — Looks like the name, with the appearance of having been a solid color that had acid dripped on it to remove some color.

Variations abound, but those are the basics. Cost increases with the number of colors and the difficulty. Shops usually like a fifty-yoyo minimum to keep costs down but if you pay more, you can get smaller numbers. Techniques other than anodizing pop up occasionally but are rare due to either cost or inconsistent results. Ten years ago, powder-coated yoyos were common, but not anymore. The volume of material added in the process introduced more imbalance than current yoyoers will tolerate.

Best Practice for Ordering Colors

1. **Provide pantone colors** — Pantone is a system of color naming that is used across many industries. I suggest a spreadsheet or document that lists the name, pantone number, a link to the pantone page, and a cut/paste of the actual color from the Pantone site.
2. **Offer examples of the technique** — If you want a particular splash pattern or fade, try to find something similar in an existing yoyo. Obviously, you aren't trying to copy another brand, but if you want really wide strips of splash, find something similar. The same applies to micro-splash or a type of acid wash.
3. **Provide engraving files** — Your design needs to be clear with very clean lines. Simpler is better — especially if a logo on the rim is going to be small.

Be very clear, and remember that anodizing is equally science and art form. Years ago, a friend who does anodizing in his garage walked me through the process as I was considering learning how to do it myself. I took pages of notes. By the end, I realized that there were just too many ways for me to make a mistake and mess it up. The parts must be perfectly cleaned, temperatures exact, time in the dye measured perfectly. The number of parts put through a single batch of dye will change the tint of the end color as the dye weakens. I've found that you can be as specific as you want, but still must be prepared for mistakes. The positive to this is that some of my best-selling colors have been mistakes. So to some degree, it all averages out.

SCALING UP

When you order a prototype you usually get 3-4 yoyos for around $300. That's something like $75 per yoyo. Obviously yoyos would be a lot more expensive if that was the actual cost of producing them. When it comes time to order a production run, one hundred parts is usually the minimum. You can order less but they are usually priced so that 100 or more makes the most sense. That quantity usually gets you two different colors (fifty pieces each). Likewise, larger numbers will generate discounts. This is where you need to do some math. Here are some very, very rough numbers representing what you might pay for 6061 aluminum yoyos manufactured in China.

50 pieces – $25-$30 per yoyo (Total $1,500)
100 pieces – $16-$20 per yoyo (Total $2,000)
200 pieces – $10-$15 per yoyo (Total $3,000)

These numbers aren't exactly what you will pay for your yoyo, but they are in the ballpark based on quotes I've received over the years. As you can see, from fifty to two hundred, twice as much money gets you four times as many yoyos. That basically means you get one hundred for free.

You can really start to see savings when you get up to five hundred in an order. I made five hundred of the Rain City Skills "Gamer" because I wanted the price low enough to sell to beginners. At five hundred pieces, the cost can go down to where it's cheaper to make five hundred than it is to make two hundred.

My understanding is that there is a difference in time for the shop. Ten orders of one hundred takes more time to fill (tinkering with the machine, switching jobs, programming, paperwork) than one order of 1,000. There is also the profit-per-sale perspective. The shop is willing to accept a lower per-unit profit if they are making more overall on your order. If they are making $500 profit on the fifty-yoyo order but $1,000 profit on a 200-yoyo order, that's twice as much profit. More importantly, that's work they can count on having. Four orders of fifty yoyos will make them more profit in theory, but just as you do with your business, they account for the extra work - tracking down customers, confirming designs, and setting up the machines and down time in between orders.

ASSEMBLY AND TESTING SERVICES

For a per-unit fee, many of the Chinese shops will assemble and box the yoyos. They will also test them. Testing is the most time-consuming part of assembly. If the halves of a yoyo are identical, and the ball bearing is precisely machined, you should be able to just screw the yoyo together and get a perfectly smooth spin. More often, you have to mix and match halves to get a matched pair. You can also "tune" them by adjusting the placement of the axle. The axle hole is generally drilled deeper than the axle, so you can have more axle in one half than the other to slightly adjust the balance.

The shop I work with currently tests the batch and discounts any vibration-related "B-grades" they find. This, in my opinion, more than pays for the assembly fee. You can save money by doing that work yourself. I've assembled well over two thousand yoyos and that's enough for me. I still personally test each yoyo and inspect for flaws. Quality control gets better and better, but I still want to assure my customers that each yoyo is up to my standards. Assembling and testing yoyos can be fun and somewhat meditative, but I prefer having the shop do it.

This is a very light summary of the process. Everything varies from project to project. Once you have your production run ordered, it's time to look at sales and put your marketing plan in action.

LOGO ART AND PACKAGING

I've talked before about the storytelling aspect of selling a yoyo. Part of that story is the presentation of the physical good. Your choice of package and logo is critical when the time comes for reviewers and early buyers to share their experience with your product. A plain brown box won't stand out, and customers will toss it in the recycling. If you use a custom-designed box and logo, it'll be kept as part of the experience, and they will post photos. Half of my marketing happens a week after the release with no added effort on my part, when the first customers receive their package and post pictures.

You can sell a yoyo without a fancy logo, but you at least need the name in stylized letters. You can create something in Photoshop if you have artistic skills and a firm grasp on what works for advertising. Otherwise, best practice is to hire a graphic designer. There is a difference between creating beautiful art and creating a logo that will help drive sales, and a professional will be able to help ensure the latter.

How do you decide what art to use? Start with your yoyo theme. The "Gamer" logo had a video game controller and a baseball cap with game logos on it representing the four colorways in the original release. The "Sk8r" had a graffiti-style skateboard drawn by a skater/artist. In both cases, I paid a professional artist. The "Convoy" featured a boat with the Rain City Skills skyline on top and the "Broke Village" shack on the back, combining the theme of the logo and the elements of both brands. We used a similar concept with the graphic for the "Space Needle Begleri" — MonkeyfingeR Design's signature gorilla wearing my fedora and yellow glasses. Most of my logos revolve around a mix of fun and serious, but you need to do what works for your brand.

Once you have a logo, keep in mind that's a piece of intellectual property that you can use again. If you work with a graphic designer, be sure to get a written contract that grants you full and exclusive rights to use the art. Then you can use it for box art, stickers, t-shirts, and a variety of advertising.

THE UNBOXING EXPERIENCE

Everyone loves getting a package in the mail. It's like the feeling you get opening a present on your birthday. Even though you know what's inside, it's still exciting. The experience is enhanced if the manufacturer has put extra effort into the experience.

Boxes in a variety of shapes and sizes can be purchased online and often from a local packaging supply store. Be creative if you want to stand out. Wood? Metal? Plastic? Origami? Whatever your choice, keep in mind three things:

1. Cost of box adds to the cost of the yoyo.

2. Heavier box equals more expensive shipping for you and for any retailers that take your product.
3. Avoid glass or fragile boxes. I made that mistake by shipping the "Hipster Highlife" in a mason jar. A couple of them ended up broken in transit. (My wife still thinks it's the coolest packaging we've used despite the shipping issues.)

That doesn't mean you shouldn't use that really cool custom wooden box you've found, just be cognizant of the added cost.

What else is going into the box? At a minimum, you need a string. A sticker is a good way to help the customer remember your brand next time they shop. Pins, sew-on patches, and temporary tattoos are solid alternatives as well. From there, the sky is the limit. I've included Lego figures, candy, extra bearings and pads, a yoyo holster, custom guitar picks, and a coloring book. Consider something like a medallion in the shape of your logo with an engraving on it, or a laser-cut wooden disk.

Whatever you decide to do to create your unboxing experience, make sure it's on theme and well crafted. What you don't want is a mess of extra stuff that just confuses the customer. You want to be remembered with excitement as a place to shop again. This makes your job easier when the time comes to make those sales.

Making the leap to ordering a production run can be intimidating. It's lot of yoyos to sell and a big expense. Keep in mind your long-term planning. Price them so they will sell, but also make sure to leave enough profit that you don't need to sell them all right away. If you can make 70% of your investment back on forty sales, you can relax a bit and let the rest move organically. It's not bad to have a previous model in stock when you release a new one; it gives new fans something else to buy when they fall in love with your newest release.

CHAPTER 16 - SALES

Your yoyos have been made, your marketing is in place, you have figured out your budget and need to price your yoyos. It's time to sell them!

PRICING

Pricing a product is a funny bit of psychology. The way people value things depend partly on how you tell them to feel. If your brand presents an image of high end, elite, and collectable, you can charge more. For example, let's take Brand X and Brand Y.

Brand X started out with simple designs, selling inexpensive but good quality yoyos at an affordable low cost. But when they tried to move into higher-end products, customers responded with statements like, "I can't justify paying $80 for a Brand X Yoyo."

At the same time, Brand Y started out with an elite, high-end item. They are able to charge three to five times more for products that cost as much to make as Brand X yoyos. They can do this because they have established customer expectations from the beginning.

This is an oversimplification, of course. Quality needs to match price, but the range of quality isn't as great as you would think. If you charge too little, people might think the quality is poor despite the opposite being true. If you charge too much you will struggle to make sales. Check out your competition fist. I started Rain City Skills aiming at the high-end collector, but have found myself in the mid-range hobbyist market because that's where I best connect with people.

There are rough price brackets when it comes to small brands.

1. At the bottom of the market, you have the brands out of China who can sell decent quality aluminum yoyos for $10–$20. This works because they make them in huge quantity (thousands at a time). They can also afford a much smaller profit margin than you because their costs are lower. That's not a place you're likely going to be competing if you are a one-person operation.

2. Next, we have the $30–$50 bracket. You may release a yoyo in this price point if you are selling direct, but be careful. If you don't convince people that this is your "Budget-friendly beginner yoyo," you can get stuck in that price range. Bigger brands dominate this price bracket because, again, they can produce larger volumes.

3. The $50–$70 price range is the most common for boutique brands. This is where you have the most room to move product fast while still covering the costs of small batches. People can generally justify a $50

impulse buy on payday — especially if your advertising is doing its job. This is where I tend to sit — in part, because I'm impatient. I could probably sell less yoyos for a higher price, but once I've released a throw, I want the funds back to make the next one!

Beyond that is grey area. This is where you get into variations on the types of material (denser aluminum, aluminum/steel hybrids, *etc.*). A Made in America yoyo usually ends up closer to the $100 price point. I've found it's challenging to charge much more than that unless you are selling titanium or providing a unique service like MonkeyfingeR's anodizing. Over the years, I've seen a few brands keep prices high through limited edition short runs. If you release only very small batches of yoyos at a time, you end up with fans willing to pay anything to grab one while they can. This is especially common with less common materials like titanium. Other brands like Oh-Yes-Yo can charge higher prices because the owner has a dedicated fan base who appreciate his artistic skills.

THE REAL COST OF MAKING YOYOS

No matter the target price bracket, understanding the total cost of business is critical in pricing your yoyo. My 2019 "12 Months, 12 Yoyos" plan revolved around each month's release, selling the minimum required for cost recovery. My strategy is to create a back-catalog of releases in stock that have sold enough to pay for the cost of the run. This inventory will provide a stream of profit as I experiment further next year. To make this work, I have to do the math of yoyo costs + business costs = $$. Then I set my price so that no more than 60% of the yoyos sold pay off my costs. This works with direct sales; with retail sales, it's closer to 80%. To even begin this math I have to understand all the costs involved.

Here's a list of factors to consider in pricing and some very, **very** general pricing for the sake of the example. These numbers assume you make two yoyo types in a year — one hundred pieces of each:

1. *Cost of prototypes + Shipping*
$500

2. Cost of production run yoyos

$4,000 (200 yoyos at $20 each after shipping)

3. Cost of yoyos sent to sponsored players + shipping

(No dollar value, this comes out of the $4000 production run)

4. Cost of advertising

Reviewers, giveaways, paid ads, any trades for graphic design
$300 (five yoyos)

5. PayPal or credit card fees on each sale

(On a $50 yoyo, you pay $0.875). You also pay fees when retailers buy from you.
$175

6. Packaging, stickers, extras

$600 ($3 per yoyo) — My costs are closer to $10 per yoyo, but I spend more than you likely will.

7. Your business overhead

(website and other subscriptions? label printer? travel costs? contest sponsorship?)
$1,000 per year ($5 per yoyo assuming two releases a year)

8. Shipping

(If you charge customers a full shipping cost, this is zero. If you discount shipping, that comes out of your sale price.)
$400 (assuming a $2 per yoyo discount on shipping costs to stay competitive)

That gives you a total cost of **$6,975, or $34.89 per yoyo**. At $50 retail, you are going to make just over $15 with direct sales. To make a profit at wholesale, you are looking at selling for $80 each (retail stores expect to double the wholesale price). Again, these are very rough numbers to make the point that costs include far more than just the cost of the parts. Companies that sell yoyos for less than $40 each through retail are either based in the countries with drastically lower costs, producing yoyos in large volume, or failing to take into account all the expenses of running a yoyo business and selling at a loss. Staying on top of the math will help your business grow and keep your stress levels under control.

DIRECT SALES OR RETAIL?

When I started yoyoing in 2009, very few brands were able to sell directly to their customers. Setting up a webstore and accepting payment was a lot more difficult than it is now. PayPal existed, but it wasn't as easy to use or it wasn't as trusted. A new yoyo brand had to rely on the few retail stores taking their yoyos. Ten years later, it takes about thirty minutes to set up a webstore connected to a PayPal account and bank account, and another fifteen minutes to set up a few products for sale.

Direct Sales

Direct sales allow you to keep your prices low, while still having enough of a profit margin. Time to take off your artist hat and put on the business hat. You need a way to collect money and organize orders. Coffin Nachtmahr of Oh-Yes-Yo somehow manages to do it all through a Facebook page and a notebook. I don't know how he does it, but he keeps track of everything.

That's fine if you are organized and have a brand or personality that will draw customers that order directly. I don't have the level of skill, so I spend the money on a webstore with a proper e-commerce setup. Earlier in this book, I covered plenty of options. I have found that you have to spend either time or money at this stage. WordPress can be free or close to it, but you are looking at dozens of hours learning how to build with it. Other sites like Shopify or Squarespace require basic computer skills and a little time to get started, but cost $15–$30 per month. For my purposes, it's worth spending this much per month to have everything collected neatly in one place, but your needs are likely different from mine.

Selling exclusively direct also allows you to keep full control over marketing. You know your costs and know when you can include extras, offer discounts, and combine products to upsell. You can set your prices a little lower and still have higher profit margins than you would get selling through a retail store. Each sale is also a direct line to a customer and a chance to ask them to sign up for your mailing list or to like/subscribe/follow on social media. These more personal connections help grow your brand.

The downside to exclusively selling direct is market access. You have to start from scratch, convincing potential customers that your webstore is trustworthy and that your product is worth buying. If you want a bit of a head start, you may consider trying to sell through retail stores.

Retail Store Sales

Selling your yoyos to a retail store instead of directly to customers has its own benefits. An established retailer has a customer base shopping specifically for yoyos. It's great advertising. A big online store has a huge audience, and their marketing budget is much bigger than yours. They spend money on advertising, which is expensive and difficult to do effectively. Customers scroll through the new release page when shopping, so your products will be seen by a lot of new potential customers.

There is an added level of trust and a wider access to the yoyo market. If you sell exclusively through retailers, the hassle of shipping and much of the customer service is out of your hands. This leaves you more time to design your next marketing campaign and next yoyo. Having your throw in a major store adds legitimacy as well. It's also an easy, trusted place for people to buy your yoyo. People can also bundle products together to save on shipping, so customers who go to the website to buy a different yoyo have a chance to impulse-buy yours.

There is also the benefit of a bulk sale. If you make four colors and the store buys five of each, that's twenty yoyos sold right away. Get three or four stores on board, and you don't have to worry about selling direct at all! The downside is that you are essentially responsible for selling your yoyos twice. You sell them to the store; then you need to make sure the store sells out.

I spent two years running my own online retail store, Return Top Shop. The experience gave me a view of the other side of the equation — the retail store selling other brand's yoyos. Every yoyo I stocked in the store was a gamble. Some sold out; others sat on the shelf. From the boutique brand owner's perspective, the markup is huge (usually double the wholesale price), but in reality, it's a tiny profit margin compared to the costs of doing business. This means that if you are going to approach retailers with your product, you need to do so with a clear plan outlining the ways you are going to help them sell any yoyos they purchase from you.

The downside is an increased retail price and a lower profit margin. Online retail stores are generally looking to double their cost. This means that if you want to sell to stores for $40, you can expect a retail store to sell it for $70–$80.

It can also be very difficult to get a yoyo into retail stores. You have a lot of competition, and stores are looking to stock yoyos that they can be sure of selling. When you contact a retailer, be prepared with a well-written piece of advertising copy. Tell the story of the yoyo, outline the details, specifications, and anything you can to point out what makes your yoyo stand out. Include well-shot and edited photos. Finally, outline in detail all the ways you plan to advertise the fact that your yoyo is in their store. You want to show them that if they stock your yoyo, you are going to move mountains to make sure they make some money.

Hybrid Sales

This refers to the increasingly common practice of selling both direct and through retail stores. My business model is to stagger the two methods. Some smaller projects I sell direct; the bigger ones I run through retail stores. This gives me the benefit of the added profit on direct sales and the brand recognition that comes with retail sales.

Two very important things to remember if you go this route: (1) promote the retailers and (2) never undercut their prices. You need to keep that relationship strong if you want to grow your business. That means you may sacrifice a direct sale to point a customer to your retailer, so that the retailer will sell out and want to buy your next yoyo. Likewise, once you've set a price, you have to stick to it, even if you think the product would sell at a lower price. You can still run occasional promotional discounts (Black Friday

— 15% off everything in the store), but don't permanently discount a product unless retailers have sold out and don't want to restock.

Selling yoyos involves far more than just making a yoyo and posting on Facebook. It's an incredibly complex and time-consuming endeavor. It takes planning, money, and a lot of hard work but it has plenty of rewards. The feeling of having created a physical thing that is in people's hands giving them joy has immeasurable value. It's a way to make connections and meet people whose path you may never have crossed otherwise. All of the marketing tools I've discussed come into play when the time comes to sell your masterpiece. If you have spent the time to build a fan base, a mailing list, and a presence in your target market, you've got a good chance of getting your yoyo into hands.

CONCLUSION

The yoyo has a long history, and a bright future. Technological innovation continues, as does the passion and skill of the players. The internet has provided wide access to share ideas and tricks and made it really easy for new yoyoers to get started and learn. There may be a lot of competition, but there are also a lot of people buying yoyos!

As I said in the beginning, this book isn't "everything you need to know about business." It's a starting point and some helpful tips and tricks. There are far more ways to do business than just the ones I've used. Other brands have had far greater success than me, using different marketing techniques. What I do works for me. I have fun and feel like what I put out into the yoyo world is valued. I was raised with a strong sense of integrity and empathy, and I bring that with me into my business. I keep my word and follow through on promises. I pay for goods and services promptly. This has put me in a position where people want to help, want to do what they can to see my vision succeed. Suppliers want to work with me to get things right, and customers come back again and again.

Likewise, it's important to me that if I offer to help someone else or work with someone, I keep my word and hold up my end of a bargain. I share this because a boutique yoyo brand usually revolves around the person at the head of it. How you approach the world around you dictates how potential customers respond.

I'm constantly learning new marketing tactics and adapting my overall strategy. My personal future holds more learning around using photo and video techniques to improve my advertising. I'm taking a course in best practices for paid ads, and I think that's going to make a big difference in the growth of Rain City Skills. My inner "grumpy old man" has a hard time getting a grip on newer social media platforms, but I'm working on getting past that.

I'm making a lot of yoyos, and more importantly I'm making a lot of friends. The yoyo community is wonderful, and I'm blessed to have found this hobby, even more so to have found a way to make a business of it that allows me to express my creativity.

So, thank you for taking the time to pick up this book. It's the first of a series and has been years in the making. I hope it has given you something to think about and perhaps even given you the push to get out there and try your hand at making your dream yoyo come true!

REVIEW AND FEEDBACK

Please leave a short review online

I hope you have found this book useful. It would mean a lot to me if you could leave an honest review online at Amazon – however short – as every bit helps. Independent authors rely on word of mouth the help new readers find our work and <u>your review can make a big difference.</u>

Feedback

Feedback from you helps me improve my writing craft. I appreciate anything you wish to share. If there is a topic I missed or an error you spot, please contact me at jdmckayauthor@gmail.com

Mailing List

Please take a moment to join my mailing list to stay informed about future releases. You can sign up at **jdmckay.com.**

Yoyos!

If this book has led you to a desire to learn how to yoyo, head to **mryoyothrower.com** for free lessons. You can also join my yoyo mailing list for weekly newsletters and discounts at my yoyo store, raincityskills.com

RECOMMENDED

READING

Books

Over the past couple years I've read a lot of books on business and marketing. There are mountains of business books out there, and I'm trying to soak up at least one a month. Here are a few that have changed my thinking and I highly recommend:

1. <u>The 4 Hour Workweek</u> by Tim Ferris – Literally the reason the book you just read exists. He talks about the value of creating intellectual property that you can keep selling, instead of products that require constand re-investment. I read that and thought "I should write a book." I liked this book because it helped me get my head into the CEO mindset. The book outlines ways to create a business, then free yourself from the running of it.
2. <u>Your Journey to Becoming Unskippable</u> by Jim Kukral – I found this book after I'd trial and error figured out a lot of his content. He presents a solid interpretation of the changes in consumerism and how to stand out in a full market.
3. <u>Newsletter Ninja</u> by Tammi Labrecque– Great guide to making the most out of your mailing list and keeping readers interested and engaged.
4. <u>Instagram For Authors</u> by Self Publishing Formula–Great breakdown of how to use Instagram for a business.
5. <u>The Tipping Point</u> by Malcolm Gladwell

Podcasts

My business growth has skyrocketed since I discovered podcasts. My best advice here is download a podcast player and start listening to business podcasts on your commute, while walking the dog, or just doing chores around the house. There are too many to list, but here are a couple I've enjoyed and learned a fair bit from.

1. The Tim Ferris Show – Top teir guests, range of topics
2. The Self Publishing Show – Focused on books, but if you skim though you'll find a lot of good tips on setting up your business and marketing.
3. TED Radio Hour – I listen to these to refocus myself and derive inspiration to get back to work.
4. Ridiculous History – Not business related, but full of weird, wild and fun history to give yourself a break from running your business!

Suggested Programs

The tools available to the online entrepreneur are mind-boggling. If you can find the right ones for you, your life will be a lot easier. Here are a few I use:

1. Canva – Simple photo manipulation software (free). Great for creating visual advertising copy. I use it primarily to create images to schedule for release to to the various social media platforms for my daily visibility posts. It has templates for most types of media you will need, from instagram stories to facebook header images.
2. Instagram Repost – There are a variety of these, test out a few and choose one that works for you. This tool allows you to share other people's Instagram posts to your gallery. I use this for reposting my sponsored players images, or fan images.
3. Hootsuite or Buffer – Programs for scheduling your social media posts. Once a week I take a bunch of photos with yoyos and use Canva to tidy them up and add captions. Then I use Hootsuite to schedule releases to Instagram, Facebook and Twitter for the week.
4. Reciept scanner – I've used Veryfi and liked it because it accuratly included taxes and produced a speadsheet of my expenses. They

increased their prices back in the fall, so I'm currently manually entering reciepts. There are a bunch of other free options, some work better than others.

5. iMovie if you are using an Apple product. It's the easiest thing for cutting together videos. There are a tonne of options PC or Andriod, find something you can use easily or want to learn.

6. Photoshop is worth getting and learning how to use, but you can do a fair bit with cheaper or free photo editing software.

7. Hemmingway Editor – Free online at hemmingwayapp.com. It's a simple but effective tool for simplifying your language in your advertising copy.

8. Mailchimp or Mailerlite – You want something to manage your mailing list.

APPENDIX A – PARTS

OF A YOYO

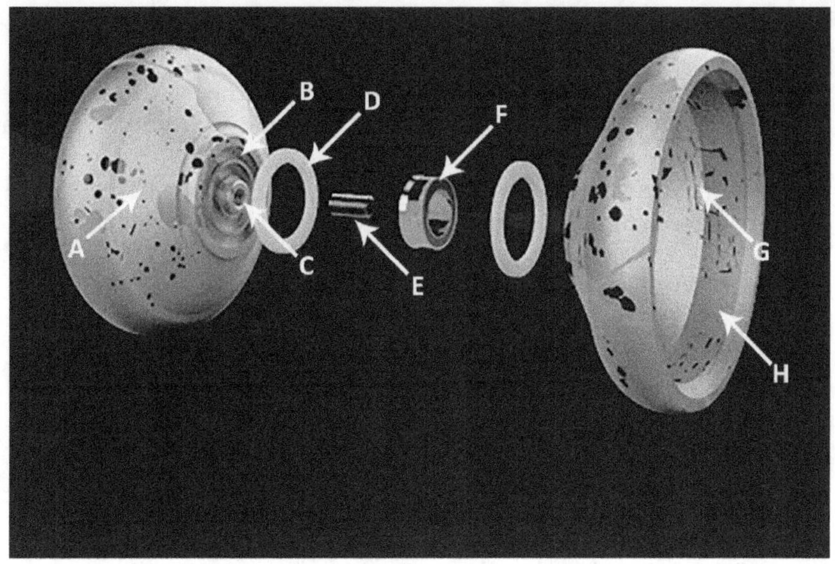

A - Gap
B - Response Groove
C - Bearing Seat
D - Response Pad
E - Axle
F - Bearing
G - Cup
H - Inner Grind Rim

APPENDIX B – STYLES

OF YOYO

Traditionally there were two styles of yoyo. 1A (for one arm) and 2A (for two arms). As players found new ways to yoyo, the naming system continued.

1. 1A – Single yoyo (usually unresponsive) attached with a single string to one hand. This is the most common style of yoyo and has an immense range of trick options
2. 2A – 2 yoyos, one attached to each hand. Tricks generally involve the yoyos looping out and in again in a variety of fashions.
3. 3A – 2 unresponsive yoyos, one tied to each hand manipulated in a more complex fashion than 2A. Yoyos are wound and tangled together in patterns, then untangled and returned to the hand.
4. 4A – The yoyo is not attached to the string. Tricks involved launching and catching the yoyo in a variety of ways. Also known as "offstring"
5. 5A – A single yoyo with a dice or similar small object (aka counterweight) tied to the end instead of a finger. The yoyo and the "counterweight" are manipulated together to create tricks.

These 5 are the standard contest divisions. There is a much longer list of trick styles that is ever evolving as players innovate. Double dragon is like 1A, but two strings are tied to a single yoyo. Full Loop is a mix of 4A and 5A, where the ends of the string are tied to make a giant loop with the yoyo unattached and manipulated with the loop. A quick search on the internet for "styles of yoyo play" will help you find the full list.

ACKNOWLEDGEMENTS

No artist operates in a vacuum. This book is the result of many, many discussions with other professionals, business owners and yo-yoers in general. It would not exist without the support of the yoyo community as a whole, members of which inspire me to keep helping the sport grow.

My wife, Andra, continues to not only tolerate my strange hobby, but revel in it. She has read this book more times than anyone should and has been extraordinarily patient as I disappear into my laptop to write "just a few more sentences."

My mom for my love of reading and passion for teaching.

My dog Dandy has also shown great patience, sitting and watching me work at the computer instead of taking him out for his 5th walk of the day.

Susan Currie for being the friend that talked me through the tought times and helped me tear the book apart and put it back together when I was stuck and ready to give up. She gave me the kick in the pants needed to keep going.

Jeyn Roberts for telling me writing about yoyos was a good idea, and slogging through my first draft and turning it into something resembling coherent thoughts.

Chris Kukucha, that teacher we all have who truly inspires and pushes us. I took five political science classes with him. He made it his priority to make sure his students not only knew the subject material, but left his class able to <u>write</u> and write well.

All of the yo-yoers who helped read through and share feedback of many drafts, I couldn't have done this without you. Paul Sarge and Waylon Crase for the help working through book cover designs as I figured out what I wanted. Stephanie Honeycutt who crafted the delightful comics at the beginning of each chapter. Cameron Blair for coming to the rescue with designs and schematics.

Did I mention my wife? Doesn't matter, she deserves double recognition.

About the Author

J.D. McKay, aka Mr. Yoyothrower, is a champion yo-yoer, an elementary school teacher, a musician and an author. He lives in Vancouver, Canada and has a small fluffy dog named Dandy (short for Yankee Poodle Dandy). He enjoys learning and sharing his knowledge. He also really likes cookies and eats far too many whilst sitting in coffee shops writing stories.

9 781999 188702